WORKWAYS OF GOVERNANCE

WORKWAYS OF GOVERNANCE

Monitoring Our Government's Health

ROGER H. DAVIDSON

Editor

GOVERNANCE INSTITUTE

BROOKINGS INSTITUTION PRESS

Washington, D.C.

Library of Congress Cataloging-in-Publication data

Workways of governance : monitoring our government's health /
Roger H. Davidson, editor.
    p.   cm.
"Sponsored by the Governance Institute."
Includes bibliographical references and index.
  ISBN 0-8157-1752-0 (cloth : alk. paper) —
  ISBN 0-8157-1753-9 (pbk. : alk. paper)
   1. United States. Congress—Evaluation.   2. Administrative agencies—United
States—Evaluation.   3. Courts—United States—Evaluation. I. Davidson, Roger H.
II. Governance Institute.

JK275.W67 2003
351.73'07'2—dc21   2003010120

9 8 7 6 5 4 3 2 1
The paper used in this publication meets minimum requirements of the
American National Standard for Information Sciences—Permanence of Paper for
Printed Library Materials: ANSI Z39.48-1992.

Typeset in Sabon

Composition by Stephen D. McDougal
Mechanicsville, Maryland

Printed by R. R. Donnelly
Harrisonburg, Virginia

Contents

Foreword

Governance is an original, enduring, and overarching subject of study at the Brookings Institution. September 11, 2001, raised profound issues about how the United States should govern itself that will reverberate for years to come. Brookings addressed some of those challenges immediately in the public activities of our scholars. Then, in Spring 2002, we brought out *Protecting the American Homeland: A Preliminary Analysis,* and in 2003 an updated edition, *Protecting the American Homeland: One Year On.*

But questions persist about the capacities of the federal agencies charged with protecting U.S. citizens: their personnel, their procedures, their working habits and styles, and their cooperation with other agencies. Insofar as these agencies fell short in a time of crisis, it was not because they had inadequate powers, policies, or even organization. It may simply have been their failure to work effectively. These qualities—what the authors whose work appears in the pages that follow call "workways of governance"—are worth serious, ongoing study.

This project, which began before September 11, addresses questions of governance that have been mounting for quite some time. The authors believe that what is needed is systematic, periodic assessment of the conditions that promote or inhibit effective performance by policymakers in the federal establishment: lawmakers, presidents and their aides, civil servants, and judges. The monitoring process would be nonpartisan and policy neutral and would embrace quantitative and qualitative fact finding and judgments. The familiar phenomenon of the periodic medical checkup is the analogy proposed by one of the authors, Federal Circuit Court Judge Frank M. Coffin. The authors note that periodic monitoring might avoid the kind of after-the-fact blame game that followed the events of 9/11.

For more than a decade, in fact, conventional wisdom has held that the federal government's working environments are deeply flawed and even dysfunctional. Mounting evidence, some systematic and some anecdotal, cannot be ignored. On Capitol Hill, members complain about the fierce partisanship that now characterizes House and Senate; many express their frustrations by retiring, often in the middle of productive and promising careers. These disappointed critics range across the political spectrum, and many of them represent safe constituencies.

In the executive branch, the operational challenges are even more urgent. White House organization has long been problematic, subject not only to the whims of chief executives but also to the vagueness of job assignments and the instability of staff management. Presidential appointees in executive branch departments have long been regarded as weak links in presidential management—especially at the subcabinet level, where the average tenure of appointees is only about two years.

The civil servants who toil in federal agencies continue to suffer what another Brookings project—the 2002–03 National Commission on the Public Service, chaired by Paul Volcker—termed a "quiet crisis." Not that federal jobs necessarily failed to inspire dedicated work. Most civil servants like their jobs and appreciate the challenge of public service. But they often chafe at their work environment: inconsistent supervision, impeding rules and regulations, poor compensation and working conditions, and, in particular, low public esteem.

As for the federal judiciary, mounting caseloads and the specter of constricted discretion and tightened resources are straining the courts' capacities, particularly at the trial level. Problems occur at both the outset and the termination of judges' careers: many would-be nominees shun the lengthy and taxing nomination and confirmation processes, and all too many leave the bench because salaries have lagged so far below the legal profession as a whole.

To explore these problems and to suggest solutions, the Governance Institute—a nonprofit, nonpartisan association of scholars and practitioners created in 1986—assembled a group of scholar-practitioners who are experts on various branches of government and who seized the opportunity to refine and test measures for their operational effectiveness. The authors identify actual and potential trouble spots, suggest ways of collecting and evaluating the evidence, and propose how to conduct periodic "checkups."

The editor of this volume is Roger H. Davidson, an emeritus professor of government and politics at the University of Maryland who has held several staff posts on Capitol Hill and has written extensively on Congress and its role in policymaking. His ties to Brookings date back to the 1960s, when he served as a research assistant and returned to write his Ph.D. dissertation as a guest scholar. Roger is the intellectual equivalent of a player-coach: in addition to editing the volume, he contributed the chapter on the U.S. House of Representatives.

The analysis of the U.S. Senate is by Sarah A. Binder, a political scientist affiliated with the George Washington University and also a senior fellow in the Governance Studies program at Brookings.

To assess White House operations, the institute enlisted two experts: Karen Hult, a political science professor at Virginia Polytechnic Institute and State University who is regarded as a pioneer in studying the organization of the presidency; and Kathryn Dunn Tenpas, who has also written on the subject and is assistant director of the University of Pennsylvania's Washington Semester Program.

The health of the federal civil service is evaluated by Paul C. Light, a Brookings senior fellow and director of its Center for Public Service.

The federal judiciary is analyzed by two distinguished judges with special insights into the character and quality of judicial workways: Judge Coffin, a senior member of the U.S. Court of Appeals, First Circuit, and Judge Robert A. Katzmann, founder and former director of the Governance Institute. Bob is also a former Brookings senior fellow and a Georgetown University professor. He now serves on the U.S. Court of Appeals for the Second Circuit and has remained close to the Institution—and, I might add, has become a valued friend and adviser to me in my first year at Brookings.

A word on the process that produced this book. The investigators presented their initial findings at a working colloquium in late 1997 at the Woodrow Wilson International Center for Scholars. The objective was to formulate ways of thinking about the problem before detailed empirical examination. The papers were subjected to a wide range of critical comment by panels of research scholars and practitioners from the legislative, executive, and judicial branches. Revised studies of the House and the Senate were aired in July 2000 at the Woodrow Wilson Center, where a large gathering of scholars and practitioners discussed in detail the preliminary findings. Finally, the draft papers were presented during a November 2001 workshop at the Brookings Institution, at which invited commentators from Brookings, local universities, and the three branches reviewed the investigators' findings.

We at Brookings are always on the lookout for partnerships with other institutions that share our mission and standards. The Governance Institute is an ideal example. Like Brookings, it explores, explains, and looks for ways of easing problems associated with the separation of powers in the American federal system; like Brookings, it probes ways in which the different levels and branches of government can better work with one another; and like Brookings, it aspires to fuse scholarship and practice, putting those who think about the policy process together with those who are part of it—to the benefit, we hope, of both groups and of the general public. Thus this book is a product of an association in which we at Brookings take particular pride.

STROBE TALBOTT
President

Washington, D.C.
April 2003

Acknowledgments

My colleagues and I at the Governance Institute are grateful for the generous support of the Pew Charitable Trusts, which underwrote the Workways of Governance Project. We are also indebted to the institutions that willingly provided venues for conferences at which we presented our preliminary findings and conclusions to diverse groups of scholars, former executives and members of Congress, and current and former staff members. The Woodrow Wilson International Center for Scholars hosted two such conferences: in October 1997 at the center's former home in the Smithsonian Castle, and in July 2000 at the center's present location in the Ronald Reagan Building. Our thanks go to Lee H. Hamilton, the center's director; Don Wolfensberger, director of the center's Congress Project; and Susan Nugent and her staff, who ably handled the arrangements.

The Brookings Institution's Governance Studies program, whose director at the time was our talented colleague Paul C. Light, provided the venue for several of our working discussions. In November 2001 Light and his staff arranged for a conference that for the final time brought our investigators together with knowledgeable experts on Congress, the presidency, the executive branch, and the courts. These individuals included Christopher Deering of George Washington University; Robert Dove, former parliamentarian of the U.S. Senate; Stephen Hess, former White House staff member and senior fellow at the Brookings Institution; Walter J. Oleszek, senior specialist at the Congressional Research Service, Library of Congress; Bradley Patterson, former White House staff member and

Brookings Institution fellow emeritus; Richard Shapiro, executive director of the Congressional Management Foundation; James A. Thurber, director of the Center for Congressional and Presidential Studies, American University; and Russell R. Wheeler, deputy director of the Federal Judicial Center. We are grateful to these individuals for their conscientious reviews of our manuscripts and for their probing suggestions concerning the courses of action we were proposing.

At Brookings, we especially want to recognize the assistance of Thomas E. Mann, former director of Governance Studies and now Averill Harriman Chair and senior fellow, who gave us valuable advice throughout, and then reviewed the final product. We appreciate, as well, the interest of the new program director, Carol Graham.

The Governance Institute's current president, Mary Graham, was helpful in the final stages of our work. The support of the institute's Board of Directors, and its treasurer, Stephen Shannon, was invaluable. John Fortier of the American Enterprise Institute helped to coordinate this project with related Pew-funded efforts.

My colleagues and I are deeply indebted to the able staff of the Brookings Institution Press. Janet Walker, managing editor of the press, oversaw the entire publication process. Art director Susan Woollen found just the right cover art to convey the book's subject matter. Janet Schilling Mowery edited the manuscripts expertly and with dispatch. Carlotta Ribar proofread the pages, and Robert Elwood prepared the index. Marketing director Becky Clark undertook the task of publicizing the book's findings. Elizabeth McAlpine provided administrative support. Robert L. Faherty, director of the press, provided personal encouragement throughout the process.

As editor, I wish, finally, to thank my colleague and friend Judge Robert A. Katzmann for his unfailing support, patience, and wise counsel throughout the project. Judge Katzmann, the founder and first president of the Governance Institute, originally conceived of this inquiry, secured the financial support, and then directed the enterprise until his confirmation as a member of the U.S. Court of Appeals for the Second Circuit. His understanding of the worlds of scholarship and governance and his personal guidance were indispensable to the successful completion of this volume.

ROGER H. DAVIDSON
Project editor

ONE   # Toward Regular Assessment of National Governmental Institutions

ROGER H. DAVIDSON

The September 11, 2001, terrorist attacks on New York's World Trade Center and government sites in Washington, D.C., raised profound questions of governance that will reverberate for many years. In this case, the government's power to act was unquestioned. Protection of their citizens is the paramount function of every government at every level; laws and ordinances conferred ample authority upon a host of protective agencies, from the U.S. military and intelligence services to the New York City fire and police departments.

The questions raised in the aftermath of the attacks were not primarily about the various governments' powers, or even about their policies. The questions that were raised centered on the agencies' capacities—their personnel, their procedures, their work habits and styles, their way of interfacing with other agencies. These are the kinds of attributes we have termed "the workways of governance."

Could the terrorist acts have been prevented by timely application of intelligence reports and surveillance? And if these attacks could not have been prevented, how many additional lives might have been spared by optimal responses from government agencies? No one knows the answers to these questions. Nonetheless, subsequent inquiries uncovered working traditions in front-line agencies—for example, the intelligence community (notably the Central Intelligence Agency and the Federal Bureau of Investigation), the Immigration and Naturalization Service, and the military commands—that severely hindered government's response to the threat of terrorism and to the event itself.[1]

The joint congressional panel named in 2002 to investigate intelligence practices before the attacks, for example, concluded that the two primary entities, the FBI and the CIA, "missed warning signals of the impending attacks and focused too much attention on threats overseas rather than on the possibility of an attack on United States soil."[2] These and other agencies, moreover, failed to process reports of terrorists' activities and communicate with one another so that the disparate clues could be placed in perspective and acted upon. (Needless to say, the targeted agencies reacted defensively: the CIA director sent an angry letter of protest to the joint committee, while the FBI tried in vain to get a court order forbidding its agents from testifying on Capitol Hill.)

The hard-won wisdom of these soul-searching inquiries was, first, that government workways are important, and indeed critical, for the nation's well-being; and, second, that defects in government operations are most readily discovered in events of crisis or scandal—all too often only after the damage has been done.

Crisis events—the attacks of September 2001 are only the most conspicuous examples—do challenge us to consider how our democratic institutions can be made to operate more effectively. However, why must we wait until a crisis has occurred to consider the capacities and performance of institutions that must deal with the challenges? To use the metaphors of students of governmental oversight, it is a question of substituting an ongoing "police-watch" review for a crisis-driven "fire-bell" response.[3] How much better would be a systematic and periodic evaluation of government agencies—a process that would attempt to measure the health of the agencies, rather than identifying the causes of some disaster that has already occurred. At the very least, such practices would minimize the finger-pointing blame game that follows governmental failures of truly tragic proportions.

Genesis of the Workways Project

The work that resulted in this volume began several years before the tragedies of September 2001. We did not embark on this enterprise with the assumption that our branches of government were necessarily corrupt or even dysfunctional. Rather, we were troubled by a growing sense that government entities at the national level had, over time, evolved into structures and developed procedures and customs that had the effect of constricting their workers' abilities and hampering their collective effectiveness. Pundits, scholars, and even public officials themselves speak candidly from time to time about their frustrations with the institutions they serve. But we were troubled by the seeming absence of systematic, ongoing, and nonpartisan evaluations of how effectively these entities work on a day-to-day basis. "The workways of governance" is the term we employ for the object of our inquiries.

How can we judge the health of our public sector institutions? How can we know when these institutions are working effectively, or when they are troubled or ineffectual? What measures of institutional health can be developed, compiled, and applied to help us make such judgments? And can such measures be used to produce periodic benchmark reports—along the lines of medical checkups or performance reviews—that will help knowledgeable outside observers, the general public, and even those inside the institutions to reach informed and balanced conclusions about the relative health and effectiveness of these institutions?

The Workways of Governance project was sponsored by the Governance Institute, a nonprofit research organization incorporated in 1986. The Institute is dedicated to exploring, explaining, and ameliorating problems associated with the separation and division of powers in the U.S. federal system. It is interested in how the levels and branches of government can best work with one another, and in how organizational problems—internal or interagency—can frustrate the functioning of government. The present effort, therefore, emerged logically from the institute's core mission. The investigators were selected for their experience and expertise in the respective national governmental institutions; their reports are collected in this volume.

A unique feature of the project is the effort to develop a periodic review of the quality of institutional life and work in government. Guidelines for evaluating and monitoring governmental entities will be established. On an annual or biennial basis (or less frequently, for some indicators), the state of each institution would be monitored and a report issued evaluating each branch. Such a monitoring process would be designed to raise the level of elite and public understanding and ultimately to serve as an agent for change in the effort to improve the capacity of government. The report would consist of both objectively measured data and subjective evaluation. Perhaps the most useful analogy was proposed by senior U.S. Circuit Court judge Frank M. Coffin: the periodic physical examination, where tests of various types, together with the physician's observations and the patient's own testimony, combine to help define the patient's status and prospects.

The Governance Institute's investigators began in 1997 by assessing, in general terms, the operational strengths and weaknesses of the chief national-level governmental entities: the House of Representatives, the Senate, the presidency, the civil service, and the federal courts. Subsequently, the investigators delved more deeply into the question of specific performance measures for the governmental branches.

Why Current Reviews Are Sporadic and Unreliable

Public understanding of the work of our national government flows in part from people's impressions of how well or poorly they provide their services. Of course, few people outside the Beltway can, or need to, master the intricacies of how government works. Yet the public benefits from a rough understanding of how laws are made, how programs are disseminated, and how legal judgments are arrived at. The public's long-term support, moreover, hinges upon an overall feeling that legislatures are capable, responsive, and ethical; that chief executives are at once resolute and flexible; that judges are fair and independent; and that government employees are accessible, sympathetic, and helpful.

Despite their obvious importance, governmental institutions are poorly understood by outsiders. The presidency is no doubt the best understood of all the national branches because a single human being, the president, is so often the focal point. Very little of the complexity of White House decisionmaking, much less of its relationships with executive agencies, penetrates the public's consciousness. Except on rare occasions—for example, the 1995 Oklahoma City bombing, the 2001 terrorist attacks, and other national disasters—federal workers are considered "faceless bureaucrats" who make things difficult for people dealing with federal agencies. Congress, with its collectivity of members, complex structure, and opaque procedures, makes it hard for people beyond Capitol Hill to grasp its character or performance. People know what judges do—though "Judge Judy" is no doubt more familiar than any of the sitting federal judges—but most of the rules and precedents that frame and underpin judicial pronouncements are beyond the average citizen's knowledge.

To the extent that these branches are judged at all, they are evaluated mainly on the basis of overall attitudes about politics, policies, and the state of the nation.[4] Do people like the way things are going, or are they worried? Are they optimistic or pessimistic about the nation's future and their own? How critical are they of politicians and other public figures? How do they regard public employees, individually and in general?

Incumbents in federal offices cannot be depended upon to convey to their constituents a sense of their institution and its workings. For example, the national legislature—and especially the U.S. House of Representatives—is the branch of government intended to be closest to the people. Yet as Richard F. Fenno Jr. found a generation ago, members of Congress typically stress their individual stewardship and try to distance themselves from the institution; they "run for Congress by running *against* Congress."[5] Evading collective responsibility for the institution's performance, representatives make it even harder for citizens to view the House as a whole. As Fenno concluded: "Representatives do very little . . . to help their supportive constituents to conceptualize the House as an institution. And if they do not encourage their constituents to think that way, the people will be much less likely to think about, much less to appreciate, the institutional strengths of the House."[6]

Nor can we rely on the communications media to convey a full-length portrait of these governmental institutions. Government agencies are not equally open and accessible to outside probing; the press, for its part, obsessively follows certain agencies and ignores many others. Congress is undoubtedly the most open of national institutions, and the House and (especially) the Senate are covered by a large and diverse press corps, local as well as national. The president is the world's most conspicuous political figure, covered by platoons of domestic and foreign correspondents. But the actual workings of the presidency—embracing the White House decision structures and their advisory networks—are opaque and closed to all but a few favored individuals, who may be provided with "leaks" calculated to advance the presidential agenda. Federal courts are covered by a small but specialized cadre of journalists; but their internal workings are famously shut to prying eyes. As for the large number of executive agencies, they range widely both in their openness to outsiders and in the level of attention accorded them by the press. Their activities are normally followed by specialized trade papers, except when scandals or disasters occur—in which case the agencies are the object of intense but inevitably fleeting scrutiny.

In any case, neither reporters nor their editors or producers can convey the elements—some of them subtle and only tangential to breaking news stories—that would point to the institutions' overall effectiveness or ineffectiveness. First, major news outlets have curtailed their coverage of national politics in general, not to mention their coverage of governmental entities.[7] Second, the focus of media coverage has shifted, with fewer stories about policy issues and more on scandal, wrongdoing, and corruption. Such stories tend only to reinforce popular negative stereotypes about these institutions.

Insofar as they pay attention to overall performance standards, the media tend to focus on rough impressions of productivity. Has Congress passed certain legislation? Are bills blocked for some reason or another? What is the level of partisan bickering or personal animosity? Do "turf wars" among federal agencies and their congressional overseers impede efficient operations? Editorials often target a "Do-Nothing Congress." The 106th Congress (1999–2001) was branded as "Still a Do-Little Congress."[8] Its successor, the 107th Congress (2001–03), came in for similar criticism. Conceding the unique series of challenges—the terrorist attacks of September 2001, the anthrax scare, the proposed Department of Homeland Security, and a proposed war with Iraq—a Capitol Hill newspaper opined that this "does not excuse the monumental act of irresponsibility now being considered by Congress' leaders: adjourning Congress and leaving vast quantities of public business simply unfinished."[9]

Those who envision a more limited role for the government might question the bias in favor of activity or productivity. But, not at all surprisingly, curtailing governmental functions demands leadership that is at least as aggressive as that required to expand government; in other words, legislative and administrative oversight are essential in either case. Exploiting the commonplace bias toward legislative productivity in terms of, say, numbers of legislative bills passed or enacted, the newly empowered Republican leadership upped the ante in 1995 by adopting a "one-hundred-days" deadline for floor consideration of the Contract with America.[10] Similar promises were made in 2002 after President George W. Bush sent to Capitol Hill his urgent but hastily conceived proposal for a new Department of Homeland Security.

In addition, academic students of government are alternative sources of insight concerning governmental performance; but they are not necessarily prepared or inclined to speak to the media and larger publics about the state of things in Washington. Liberal reformism was a strong component of the political science profession in its early years, when it was associated with progressive-era reforms and public administration's "one best way" of organization and management. This reformist commitment has faded with the rise of "scientific" research utilizing a wide variety of concepts and methodologies. It has been more than fifty years, for example, since the American Political Science Association took the initiative of issuing detailed reports and recommendations concerning party government and Congress, actions not likely to be repeated anytime soon.

Individual scholars have participated in evaluation and reform efforts in the recent past. One thinks, for example, of the several congressional reorganization panels of the 1970s, the National Commission on the Public Service (the Volcker Commission) in the late 1980s, the Clinton administration's "Reinventing Government" initiatives of the 1990s, multiple studies of presidential transitions and the presidential appointment and confirmation processes, and evolving debates over campaign finance reform. Several contributors to this volume have participated in such efforts. Invariably such investigations produce much useful information and a valuable public record, but because there is rarely much follow-up, their products all too often leave historical benchmarks rather than a continuous stream of data. And what about the handful of relevant "public intellectuals," usually scholars familiar with public sector operations and politics (whether the specialty is the presidency, Congress, the judiciary, or public management) who are intimately involved with the Washington community and who are skillful communicators to the press and the public? To be sure, these individuals sometimes address questions of institutional health; but far more often they are asked merely to comment on breaking news events or transitory phenomena.

To sum up, national government entities and their personnel have only weak incentives to concentrate on questions of the institutions' health and performance, and even fewer incentives to communicate their judgments to clients or constituents. And if the government were to devote more systematic attention to its institutional health, its findings would in all probability be highly politicized and lack general credibility beyond the Beltway. Nor can we expect the usual sets of informational gatekeepers—journalists and scholars—to be able to fill the gap in public understanding, at least on a continuing basis.

Intellectual Challenges of Evaluations

Implementing periodic appraisals raises difficult questions of measuring institutional attributes and translating the findings into understandable rankings. This is a challenge whatever the subject of the study, whether it be a school or a local government or the U.S. Congress. Fortunately for evaluative purposes, these are public bodies; they generate large numbers of identifiable and measurable products, and they have been studied systematically for many years. In thinking about how to establish periodic evaluations, therefore, we have sizable bodies of information to aid us.

One option, albeit controversial and perhaps extreme, lies in the burgeoning practice of organizational (or institutional) report cards. This device has been defined by William Gormley and David Weimer as: "a regular effort by an organization to collect data on two or more other organizations, transform the data into information relevant to gauging performance, and transmit the information to some audience external to the organizations themselves."[11] Such evaluations, whether they take the form of report cards or follow some other format, are not self-generated but are compiled and transmitted by independent entities. Of necessity, however, they rely in part on information supplied by subjects of the evaluation. Second, many such evaluations translate the collected data into "grades" (ratings or rankings) that compare performance among organizations or in terms of a definable set of standards. Third, translating the data into simplified form enables external audiences (journalists, consumers, citizens) to interpret the findings and perhaps act upon them. Indeed, the mass media have been all too quick to see the advantages of such devices.[12]

Reporting and ranking mechanisms of this type are familiar, though not always beneficial, parts of our commercial and even political landscape. Comparative rating schemes have long been familiar in the commercial world, from the Good Housekeeping Seal of Approval to systematic product testing (Consumers Union) and product user surveys (J. D. Power and Associates). Policy analysts, industry analysts, and other users of large databases also find rating schemes useful. Newspapers and magazines increasingly produce report cards or quality ratings concerning various subjects. Professional groups adopt them in order to promote and regulate qualification and performance standards. Recently the concept has traveled to the realm of public or private social services such as schools, training facilities, physicians, hospitals, HMOs, and airline safety and performance. State and local governments are also subjects of various rating devices.

Our project authors reject simplistic formulas that rely on a limited range of measures upon which are hung a string of grades or scores. Such rating schemes are necessarily reductionist; that is, they are based on limited and usually readily quantifiable variables. Lists of the "best" colleges and universities, for instance, are faulted because they are weighted toward a small number of variables (for example, faculty salaries or class sizes) that may or may not be important to a particular student searching for a college. Subjecting governmental entities to periodic examinations therefore demands that the widest range of measures be employed: quantitative data, to be sure, but also qualitative information gleaned from, say, interviews, case studies, and judgments of informed observers.

At least two elements of reporting identified by Gormley and Weimer might serve as guidelines for evaluations of the type we envision. First, evaluations must be prepared independently of the institution being examined (however much these reports may draw upon information generated by that institution). Second, the evaluations—however complex and multifaceted they may be—must be reported in a form that can be conveyed succinctly and meaningfully to concerned publics: those within the institution itself, the institution's clients, the press, and ultimately the general public.

In applying the concept of periodic evaluations to branches of the federal government, there arises also the question of comparability. The U.S. government is unique in many respects, even among nations that follow our constitutional model. The Senate and House of Representatives, by the same token, exhibit many prerogatives and practices that set them apart from, say, state assemblies or parliaments throughout the world. The comparability problems are far from unsolvable, however. Although the rankings themselves would apply solely to the given institution, instructive comparisons can be made both in gathering data and in translating those data into understandable packages. The same can be said of chief executives, bureaucracies, and national courts. First, in a number of specific respects U.S. governmental entities can fairly be compared with parallel entities in the states and in other nations. The U.S. Senate and House of Representatives, for example, share certain specific attributes with other legislative bodies such as state legislatures and representative assemblies in other nations. Second, longitudinal data offer opportunities to compare institutions over time, to identify and reflect upon organizational trends. Finally, the Workways of Governance Project envisions a set of roughly comparable, though certainly not identical, standards that might be applied to various government entities: the White House, presidential appointees, the civil service, and the courts, as well as the houses of Congress. However disparate their structures and constitutional mandates, these entities share attributes and capacities found in all formal organizations: for example, personnel; communications networks; output measures; and modes of identifying problems, processing information, and reaching decisions.

Another potential problem of such evaluations surrounds their expected effects upon the targeted institutions themselves as well as the affected publics. Evaluations, of course, are meant to affect the behavior of the institutions they evaluate, as well as the behavior of their relevant publics, be they clients, consumers, funding sources, or the general public. Even more problematic, targeted agencies may respond by devoting their resources to remedying the faults identified by the rating scheme, to the exclusion of other goals that may be in the institution's overall interest. To continue the educational analogy, administrators eager to polish a college or university's ranking oftentimes resort to hiring a string of "star" professors, a costly course of action that may have minimal classroom impact and unintended consequences, such as lowering the morale of existing faculty members. Our response to this problem is to propose a wide range of evaluative indicators—qualitative as well as quantitative—including time-line data that show trends as well as current performance. Such a multifaceted approach would minimize any distortions resulting from the findings.

Monitoring the Branches of Government

The scholar-analysts represented in this volume have attempted to apply these general guidelines to evaluations of the leading institutions of the federal government: the House of Representatives, the Senate, the presidency (focusing on White House organization and staffing), the executive branch (focusing on the civil service), and the federal judiciary. This ordering is not arbitrary; it follows the first three articles of the Constitution: Congress comes first, then the executive, and finally the judiciary. Naturally, it is also the scheme followed by the authors of *The Federalist*, still the most authoritative description of what the writers of the Constitution thought they had brought into being. (Their discussions of the executive branch, albeit relatively brief, were subsumed under the topic of the powers of the chief executive.) Unlike Madison, Hamilton, and Jay, we are trying to grasp the complexities of entities boasting more than two centuries of maturation and institutionalization. Therefore our examination of their workways brings us to strikingly different points of departure and sets of questions. Nonetheless, we hope our investigations reflect in some small degree the same qualities of high-mindedness and shrewd practicality displayed by the authors of *The Federalist*.

Evaluating the House of Representatives

There is of course no perfect or ideal legislative body. First, there is considerable disagreement over what constitutes a healthy legislature.[13] Some, for example, might value a cautious and deliberate body, while others might prefer a chamber that moves expeditiously in the face of pressing demands and need. Second, not all the criteria we would expect of a healthy institution are necessarily compatible with one another. Can a legislature be both efficient and deliberative, or does securing one attribute harm the prospects of achieving the other? Third, even if we agreed upon the standards of a healthy body, devising objective criteria with which to gauge the institution would prove extremely difficult. What does a "representative" body look like? What is the mark of a "deliberative" or an "efficient" body? Numerous scholars and commentators have debated these points, and they have rarely reached common ground.[14]

Although such debates may seem arcane and academic to the policymaking community in Washington, we see a pressing need for a systematic evaluation of the House and Senate. Historically, there have been waves of concern about the House and its proceedings; and "congressional reform" has proved a salient topic for civic-minded critics and observers for at least several generations. What is needed is ongoing observation of the institution, one that begins not with reformist premises but with searching questions about institutional workways and how to judge their results.

In the early days, proceedings at the Capitol were relatively casual and often disorderly, especially in the House. As the institution matured, however, decorum by and large replaced chaos, and stricter rules of order came to govern the proceedings. Today the House is governed by a formidable array of rules and precedents, as well as numerous informal norms and traditions. Altering the proceedings is not a casual matter. (The Senate, as a continuing body, has rules that may be modified only by a two-thirds vote. However, the House, whose membership turns over every two years, adopts its rules anew when each new Congress convenes.)

Despite institutional inertia, the House and Senate have repeatedly adapted their ways of doing things, partly in reaction to altered partisan or factional alignments, partly to accommodate shifts in membership. Most major changes in House rules and proceedings have resulted from concerted effort by the leadership, party caucuses, and the Rules Committee. When major rules changes or committee jurisdictional realignments are considered, select committees are often employed. Since World War II at least ten formal reorganization committees or study commissions have been created, the most recent in 1993.

Not all institutional changes have been visible to the general public. Incremental changes of one kind or another are common. For example, the House in 1999 streamlined and codified its rules, and hardly anyone noticed. Scholars have argued that periodic, large-scale "reform acts" aimed at revising committee jurisdictions and procedures are mainly compilations of gradually accumulated precedents created as new types of bills were introduced.[15]

Evaluating the Senate

The case of the Senate is even more urgent, if we are to heed the recent critiques of outside observers and even of senators themselves. In the 1990s and early 2000s, numerous senators—a distressing proportion of whom would be regarded as especially valuable members—departed the chamber expressing dissatisfaction and disappointment with their experience of serving in the body. As Warren Rudman asked upon leaving the Senate, "Why are outstanding people leaving who could serve in the Senate another decade or two? . . . Most [of the ones I've talked to] are leaving because the Senate has become so partisan, so frustrating, and so little fun."[16] Several senators have contemplated leaving the Senate to run for governor in their home states. Far from seeing state service as a lesser calling than national office, these seasoned legislators suggest that their ability to have a direct impact on social and economic lives would be far greater in the state capital. To be sure, many senators continue to serve with few misgivings about their experiences on Capitol Hill. But the fact that politicians inside and outside so often bemoan the nature of lawmaking in the Senate suggests that an investigation of the chamber's workways is in order.

Despite the intricacies of constructing a checkup for the Senate, Workways author Sarah Binder boldly took up the task of attempting to devise such a test. In the process, she consulted broadly with former members, legislative scholars, and seasoned Hill staff.[17] In some ways these consultations simply reinforced for us the difficulty of crafting a suitable checkup for the Senate. Few believed, for example, that a single set of standards could be applied to the House and Senate, which have distinct constitutional duties and organizational attributes. But those we consulted did agree that what is ultimately important is the Senate's legislative performance. Did the Senate respond to pressing problems and do its part to provide policy solutions to the nation's major problems? Our consultations, in order words, hit home for us the importance of focusing on output: that is, how well the chamber responds to the issues of the day.

In devising a health checkup for the Senate, Binder focuses on the chamber's ability to set its agenda and move itself to make major policy decisions. For an ordinary legislature, we might think that this sets the bar too low. But the Senate, of course, is no ordinary legislative body, as reflected in the traditional senatorial belief that they are custodians of "the greatest deliberative body in the world." Cautious, deliberate—these are the words defenders of the institution employ to explain the Senate's slow-moving character. Given the Senate's appetite for lengthy debates and its rules that permit minorities to determine the pace of the body's deliberations, holding the Senate to a different standard of performance might place unfair expectations on it.

Thus instead of evaluating the Senate's speed or efficiency, we focus on the ways in which the Senate typically moves toward making decisions, and evaluate how well and how often the Senate completes these tasks of decisionmaking. How long does it take to negotiate time agreements under which the Senate will debate major bills? How many cloture motions are filed on major bills? What is the Senate's record in completing action on these major and salient measures? By surveying the decisionmaking landscape of the Senate, we hope to craft an institutional checkup that both appreciates the unique character of the Senate and holds the Senate up to reasonable yet ambitious standards of legislative capacity and effectiveness.

Evaluating the Presidency

As an individual, the U.S. president is undoubtedly the most conspicuous public official in the world. Nearly everyone knows the president's name; most U.S. citizens, and sizable numbers of people in other countries, can express judgments about his personality and performance. Indeed, since the late 1930s, popular rankings of presidential job performance have been the most frequently repeated items in public opinion surveys.[18] Even some aspects of presidents' "workways," within the definition of this volume, are widely reported in the press: for example, their work habits, decisionmaking routines, travels, vacations, and personal styles.

The contemporary presidency, however, is far larger and more complex than the president's personal, visible image. Organizationally, the White House Office (WHO) and its larger entity, the Executive Office of the President (EOP), employ several thousand people (the exact number is questionable) and embrace complex organizational and personal relationships. To be sure, presidents are not elected for their skills at marshalling aides and leading organizations; but these skills, as often as not, determine the success of their presidencies. And it is very difficult for people outside the White House orbit—much less those far from the nation's capital—to grasp the complexity of presidential decisionmaking or to appreciate how the structure and operations of the White House staff can facilitate or constrain presidential performance. Yet White House management matters a great deal: close observers of the presidency point, for example, to the operational effectiveness achieved under such chiefs of staff as James Baker III and Howard Baker (during Ronald Reagan's presidency) and Leon Panetta (during Bill Clinton's presidency).

For much of the history of the presidency, staffing was a haphazard matter; assistance was gleaned from relatives or personal associates, who typically received very little compensation. The need for presidential assistance beyond such makeshift arrangements swelled to crisis proportions when the federal New Deal programs of the 1930s stretched executive capacities beyond their traditional boundaries. "The president needs help," declared the Brownlow Committee, created by Franklin D. Roosevelt after his first reelection. "His immediate staff is entirely inadequate."[19] Among the group's recommendations implemented by Roosevelt was creation of the White House Office within a larger entity, the Executive Office of the President.

Since Roosevelt's time, the White House staff has grown in size and become more specialized. But when the presidency and its staff do receive attention, it is often only *after* serious problems have arisen in which the White House or the president is directly implicated (such as the Bay of Pigs and Cuban Missile Crisis in John F. Kennedy's administration; Watergate in Richard Nixon's; the Bert Lance controversy in Jimmy Carter's; the Iran-contra affair in Reagan's; and multiple controversies in Clinton's). The responses of outside critics, moreover, have frequently missed the mark.

President Dwight D. Eisenhower's national security decisionmaking system, for example, was faulted for being "too formal," leading to congressional hearings and a major overhaul of the National Security Council system by Kennedy, his successor. Yet following the 1961 Bay of Pigs fiasco, Kennedy restored some of the old procedures. Later, presidential scholars would argue that Eisenhower's decisionmaking was actually enhanced by his reliance on both formal and informal structures and procedures.[20]

The post-Watergate critique of the White House—that President Nixon had introduced a "swollen staff" that ran amok and isolated the president—generated an immediate effort by Gerald Ford and subsequent electoral promises to cut the size of the White House staff. However, efforts to address allegedly oversized staffs, although politically popular, produced some harmful (and often deceptive) staff "cuts" in the Ford, Carter, and Clinton presidencies, many of which were soon reversed.

"Since the Kennedy administration," John P. Burke notes, "presidents have received, solicited and unsolicited, a range of advice on organizing their White House staffs."[21] Indeed, this has become a virtual cottage industry, producing a range of materials from distinguished scholars and practitioners.[22] Despite all of these efforts, Burke finds scant evidence of either "an upward learning curve" in drawing on the institutional resources of the presidency or "as much stock-taking from the mistakes or difficulties (or, in some cases, successes) of predecessors as might make the task easier and more effective."[23]

The Workways project essay (chapter 4), written by Kathryn Dunn Tenpas and Karen Hult, highlights the importance of increased public access and ongoing systematic attention to presidential advisory systems. The focus is upon these systems' contributions both to advancing presidential objectives ("effectiveness") and to addressing the concerns and requests of the president and other members of the Washington community ("responsiveness"). The authors note that the presidency differs in key respects from Congress and even the federal courts in providing public access to information and to decisionmakers themselves. The George W. Bush administration's habits of secrecy, not to mention the post-9/11 political environment as a whole, make this an even greater concern.

Evaluating the Federal Work Force

The federal bureaucracy, which lies largely within the executive branch, is given scant attention in the Constitution. As Leonard D. White recalls in his classic study of early executive operations:

The Constitutional Convention had displayed a notable lack of interest in the organization of the executive branch, apart from the office of the Chief Magistrate. It was assumed . . . that there would be departments to handle the foreign affairs of the country, the army, and the fiscal business. There was no debate concerning the number, powers, responsibility, or duties of the heads of departments. They were barely recognized in the Constitution in the phrase authorizing the president to secure their opinions in writing.[24]

Nonetheless, a sizable federal establishment was surely envisioned as an essential ingredient of an "energetic" executive. The very first Congress (1789–91) began to shape the executive branch by passing laws establishing three executive departments and filling in details of the president's supervisory authority. The puny executive force that President George Washington inherited from the existing apparatus under the Articles of Confederation soon began to expand, slowly at first, but more rapidly during times of war and crisis. The post–Civil War era brought broader governmental functions, which were augmented during the years of Woodrow Wilson's New Freedom agenda, Franklin D. Roosevelt's New Deal agencies and programs, and the Great Society legislation of the 1960s and 1970s. Before the outbreak of World War II, federal civilian employment stood at 699,000; by 1945 it had grown to 3.37 million—the highest level ever.[25]

Growth is not limited to periods of expansive presidential and congressional policymaking. President Reagan, who pledged to eliminate two cabinet departments, failed to achieve that goal and ended up creating an additional department (Veterans Affairs). During his presidency the federal civilian payroll grew by more than 200,000 workers, most of them in defense-related agencies.[26] After the 2001 terrorist attacks, President George W. Bush acted to expand military capacity and proposed a new Department of Homeland Security of some 170,000 employees, not all of them transfers from existing agencies. In 2001, the most recent year for which we have data, the federal civilian workforce stood at 1.8 million.[27] To these figures should be added those working for government contractors or industries dependent upon federal largesse.

Historically, different philosophies have governed policymakers' attitudes toward the nature and quality of the federal work force. The Federalists seemed to prefer an elite corps drawn from the ranks of "the rich and the wise and the well-born." Thomas Jefferson and his followers placed their confidence in a natural aristocracy of talent and skills. Andrew Jackson and his followers established what came to be known as the spoils system: awarding government jobs to party loyalists. Subsequent presidents spent many of their waking hours receiving and interviewing federal job seekers. The Pendleton Act of 1883—passed in part as a reaction to the assassination of President James Garfield by a disgruntled office seeker—established a graded civil service system of workers chosen for their skills and promoted according to performance.

Civil service standards spread throughout the government's agencies, producing a federal work force that was theoretically based on skills and not on political leanings. But presidents and political managers began to worry about their loss of leverage over the bureaucracy: How could federal agencies be made more responsive to presidentially directed policy shifts resulting in part from electoral results? How could policymakers motivate civil servants who enjoyed job security? Thus since the 1950s more attention has been paid to enlarging the cadres of political appointees and to permitting greater flexibility in dealing with top-level civil servants. For example, the critical issue surrounding George W. Bush's proposed Homeland Security Department was the president's insistence on flexibility to bypass traditional civil service rules in hiring/firing and promoting/demoting its employees.

The term "quiet crisis" has been employed to characterize the contemporary state of the federal work force. The term was originally coined by public administration scholars Roslyn Kleeman and Charles Levine to describe the slow weakening of the public service in the 1970s and 1980s.[28] Despite a comprehensive attempt to revitalize the service through the Civil Service Reform Act of 1978, the situation had deteriorated by 1987, when the National Commission on the Public Service was convened by its chair, former Federal Reserve Board head Paul Volcker. "This erosion has been gradual, almost imperceptible, year by year," the Volcker Commission concluded. "But it has occurred nonetheless."[29] Not since the rise of the spoils system in the Jacksonian era did civil servants have such good reason to feel beleaguered.

The Volcker Commission found that the federal work force suffered from neglect and disparagement. The public had lost confidence in their elected and appointed leaders, and no wonder: "bureaucrat bashing" by the media and political candidates was at an all-time high. Morale within the civil service was at a modern low. The gap between federal and private pay was widening, and the Office of Personnel Management (OPM) was run by a director who believed that mediocre workers were good enough for government. Not that the nation's best and brightest young people ranked government service high on their list of career choices; even if they wanted a federal job, most had no idea how to get one. As the commission put it: "Too many of the best of the nation's senior executives are ready to leave government, and not enough of its most talented young people are willing to join. This erosion in the attractiveness at all levels, most specifically in the federal civil service—undermines the ability of government to respond effectively to the needs and the aspirations of the American people, and ultimately damages the democratic process itself."[30]

Drawing on a host of data, both anecdotal and systematic, the Volcker Commission divided the quiet crisis into three components: erosion of public trust; recruitment of talented young people for public service careers; and barriers to high performance in government. In other words, improving the public service was seen as requiring a combination of better leadership, more internal capacity, and stronger incentives for performance. The federal government could not hope to regain public confidence without talented, ethical leadership, which in turn would lead to a work force staffed with America's best and brightest young people, who in turn would be given clear signals of the need for competitive performance.

To implement this model of public service, the Volcker Commission generated forty-four recommendations, roughly one-fourth of which were eventually adopted.[31] On leadership, the commission urged a decentralization of government management, a one-third cut in the number of presidential appointees, and a renewed commitment to ethical conduct. On recruitment, it argued for national service, new outreach programs, and a simplification of the federal government's complicated personnel system. On performance, it recommended competitive pay in return for competitive performance alongside a strengthening of OPM and expanded training opportunities. It also recommended creating a pay comparability system linked to differences in local cost-of-living pressures.

The Volcker Commission's findings and recommendations established a benchmark for thinking about the workways of executive branch employees. Paul C. Light illuminates the current status of the federal work force in chapter 5 of this volume, primarily by means of recent survey data on federal employees. This descriptive material will lead to a more theoretical discussion of the positive conditions needed for public servants to fulfill their roles in what Alexander Hamilton termed "a government well executed."[32]

From his investigations, Light is able to chart a course for periodic measurement of the health of the public service. But of all the unfulfilled recommendations of the Volcker Commission, undoubtedly the most important remains the one that appeared at the top of their list: presidents, their chief lieutenants, and Congress must articulate early and often the necessary and honorable role that public servants play in the democratic process, while at the same time making clear that they will demand the highest performance from those who hold the public trust.

Despite occasional progress in lifting the image of the public service, most notably in the "Reinventing Government" campaign led by Vice President Al Gore, the reality remains that government workers are an easy target of media and political attack. When in doubt, or so it seems, the easiest course for political candidates is to run against Washington and its "bureaucrats," even if the candidate is an incumbent, and even if the incumbent is the occupant of the Oval Office. Tellingly, as Light reports, survey researchers have not yet found a survey question about trust in government that generates a positive response from the public.

Evaluating the Federal Judiciary

The federal judiciary, the subject of the third article of the U.S. Constitution, is created politically but must function independently. On the one hand, the federal judicial structure, only vaguely sketched by the Constitution, is largely a creature of laws passed by Congress. Moreover, federal judges are nominated by the president and approved by the Senate. On the other hand, members of the judiciary, once in office, are to proceed impartially and in a nonpartisan fashion; they enjoy life tenure and can be removed only by the cumbersome process of impeachment.[33]

The task of judging requires both decisional and institutional autonomy. If justice is to be dispensed fairly, efficiently, and wisely, then judges must have (1) the time to devote to their responsibilities, both adjudicative and administrative; (2) the resources to discharge these responsibilities; and (3) the authority, within reasonable limits and with appropriate accountability, to manage their own affairs, free of the possibility of political retribution. Thus time, resources, and self-governance are critical elements of independent decisionmaking. They are also essential components of the optimal conditions for judging. To these, say the authors of chapter 6, must be added work that is both challenging and satisfying.

These authors, Federal Circuit Court judges Frank M. Coffin and Robert A. Katzmann, believe that a multifaceted inquiry can aid in gauging the conditions for effective judging and the health of the federal judiciary. Among the elements to be considered are: recruitment, compensation, workload volume and character, resources, time, resignations, working relationships, security, external institutional relations (Congress and the executive), public understanding, and media coverage. Some of these factors are more amenable to measurement than others. However, Judges Coffin and Katzmann believe that quantitative analysis is of only limited value for their purposes. Rather, they contend that periodic qualitative (but carefully crafted) inquiries, making use of quantitative data where appropriate, are more likely to bear fruit.

The periodic review, like the periodic physical examination, would involve several steps. First would be a deliberately unfocused questioning of a sample of judges. The respondents would be encouraged to discuss such matters as which portions of their work they found most and least rewarding or satisfying, how they spend their time, and what changes they think would improve the functioning of the judiciary.

The second step would require sifting these responses in order to create a more precise questionnaire. In such a survey judges could, for example, be asked to rank the severity of sources of frustration both within and outside the judiciary, to indicate their preferences for proposed improvements, and to offer their views about compensation and its effects on attracting able people to the bench and retaining them.

The third step would entail a series of focused discussions—perhaps as individual circuit conferences or workshops—based on the responses gleaned from the first two steps of the process. The objective would be to explore the types of improvements that might be made within and outside the judiciary. As a final step, specific innovations would be implemented insofar as they were possible or practicable.

As part of their inquiry, the authors undertook the first two steps of the evaluation process. Their survey of federal judges yielded a rich mine of data, reported in chapter 6. Regarding the link between compensation and recruitment/retention, the survey indicated that, if they knew that pay raises or regular cost-of-living increases were *not* forthcoming over the next ten years, more than six out of ten of the responding circuit and district judges would not have applied, or would have been less likely to apply, for their positions. As a way of showing the kind of practical steps that might be taken to alleviate the problems identified, Judges Coffin and Katzmann focus on a principal dilemma of the task of judging: "too much work, not enough time." They argue that the suggestion that judges "learn to work more efficiently" has the virtue of not requiring any ambitious institutional undertaking. In considering how to handle the workload with more modulated investments of time, the authors suggest that the most promising initial step would be to draw upon the reservoir of judicial self-help. They explore how the judiciary might institutionally facilitate a process whereby judges could pass on their experience and wisdom to other judges. The authors conclude that periodic checkups, self-examination, self-help, and sharing experiences would be at once preservative and renewing. They would help ensure the continuing vitality of the judiciary by equipping its human component, the individual judge, to live up to the challenge of enduring excellence.

Notes

1. Attention focused on the CIA, the FBI, and the military intelligence agencies, whose approach to antiterrorist activities was generally sluggish, standoffish, and bureaucratically insular. No doubt their responses were mirrored by other agencies. The story is recounted in detail by Daniel Benjamin and Steven Simon in *The Age of Sacred Terror* (Random House, 2002).

2. David Johnson and James Risen, "Panel's Findings Take Intelligence Officials by Surprise," *New York Times*, September 29, 2002, p. 13.

3. See Joel D. Aberbach, *Keeping a Watchful Eye: The Politics of Congressional Oversight* (Brookings, 1990).

4. Glenn R. Parker and Roger H. Davidson, "Why Do Americans Love Their Congressmen So Much More than Their Congress?" *Legislative Studies Quarterly* 4 (February 1979), pp. 53–61.

5. Richard F. Fenno Jr., *Home Style: House Members in Their Districts* (Little, Brown, 1978), p. 168.

6. Ibid., p. 246.

7. Stephen Hess, "The Decline and Fall of Congressional News," in Thomas E. Mann and Norman J. Ornstein, eds., *Congress, The Press, and the Public* (American Enterprise Institute / Brookings, 1994), pp. 141–56.

8. "Still a Do-Little Congress," Editorial, *Washington Post*, July 10, 2000, p. A10.

9. "Abdication," *Roll Call*, September 23, 2002, p. 4.

10. James G. Gimpel, *Fulfilling the Contract: The First 100 Days* (Boston: Allyn & Bacon, 1996), p. 29.

11. William T. Gormley Jr. and David L. Weimer, *Organizational Report Cards* (Harvard University Press, 1999), p. 3.

12. Ibid., p. 6.

13. Alan Rosenthal, "The Good Legislature: Getting beyond 'I Know It When I See It,'" *Legislative Studies Section Newsletter* (July 1998) (www.apsanet.org %Elss/Newsletter/jul98/rosenthal.html).

14. Malcolm Jewell, "Political Dimensions of a 'Good Legislature,'" in ibid.; Rosenthal, "The Good Legislature."

15. See David C. King, *Turf Wars: How Congressional Committees Claim Jurisdiction* (University of Chicago Press, 1997).

16. Warren B. Rudman, *Combat: Twelve Years in the U.S. Senate* (Random House, 1996), p. 254. See also John Rosenberg, "Why More Senators Are Eyeing Governor's Races, *The Hill*, October 31, 2001, p. 25.

17. See, for example, "Assessing Congress: Drafting an Institutional Report Card," workshop sponsored by the Governance Institute and the Woodrow Wilson International Center for Scholars (July 24, 2000), conference transcript.

18. For a scholarly compilation and analysis, see Paul Brace and Barbara Hinckley, *Follow the Leader* (Basic Books, 1992).

19. President's Committee on Administrative Management, *Administrative Management in the United States* (Government Printing Office, 1937), p. 3.

20. Fred I. Greenstein, *The Hidden-Hand Presidency: Eisenhower as Leader* (Basic Books, 1982); and John P. Burke and Fred I. Greenstein, with the collaboration of Larry Berman and Richard Immerman, *How Presidents Test Reality: Decisions on Vietnam, 1954 and 1965* (Russell Sage Foundation, 1989).

21. John P. Burke, *The Institutional Presidency: Organizing and Managing the White House from FDR to Clinton* (Johns Hopkins University Press, 2000), p. 24.

22. Richard Neustadt's memorandums to Kennedy before he took office survive as a model of the genre. See, for example, Stephen Hess, "Advice for a President-Elect, 1976–77," in Hess's *Organizing the Presidency*, 2d ed. (Brookings, 1988); Benjamin W. Heineman and Curtis Hessler, *Memorandum for the President: A Strategic Approach to Domestic Affairs in the 1980s* (Random House, 1980); National Academy of Public Administration, *A Presidency for the 1980s* (NAPA, 1980). In 2000 there were several major reports by, among others, the Brookings Institution, the American Enterprise Institute, the Center for the Study of the Presidency, and the Heritage Foundation.

23. Burke, *The Institutional Presidency*, p. xiii.

24. Leonard D. White, *The Federalists: A Study in Administrative History* (Macmillan, 1948), p. 26.

25. *Budget of the United States Government—Historical Tables* (Government Printing Office, 2002), pp. 298–99.

26. U.S. Bureau of the Census, *Statistical Abstract of the U.S., 2001* (Government Printing Office, 2001), table 483, p. 320.

27. *Budget—Historical Tables*, p. 299.

28. Charles H. Levine and Roslyn S. Kleeman, "The Quiet Crisis in the American Public Service," reprinted in Patricia W. Ingraham and Donald F. Kettl, *Agenda for Excellence: Public Service in America* (Chatham House, 1990), p. 3.

29. National Commission on the Public Service, *Leadership for America: Rebuilding the Public Service* (1989), p. 3.

30. *Leadership for America*, p. 1.

31. See Paul C. Light, *The Tides of Reform: Making Government Work, 1945–1995* (Yale University Press, 1997), for a discussion of the relative success of past improvement efforts.

32. Alexander Hamilton, *Federalist* No. 70, in Hamilton, James Madison, and John Jay, *The Federalist Papers* (Mentor ed., 1961), p. 423.

33. Although impeachment may be frequently threatened, it is rarely employed. Of the fifteen Senate trials (most recently that of President Clinton in 1998), only seven individuals have been convicted and removed from office. Interestingly, all seven who were removed from office were judges, who otherwise enjoy open-ended terms of office.

TWO

The House of Representatives: Managing Legislative Complexity

ROGER H. DAVIDSON

> Like a vast picture thronged with figures of equal prominence and crowded with elaborate and obtrusive details, Congress is hard to see satisfactorily and appreciatively at a single view and from a single stand-point. Its complicated forms and diversified structure confuse the vision, and conceal the system which underlies its composition. It is too complex to be understood without an effort, without a careful and systematic process of analysis.
>
> —*Woodrow Wilson, 1885*

What would a successful House of Representatives look like? Or rather, what indicators or measures would tell us most about the health of the institution and the productivity of its members and staff? Such measures must tap attributes that enhance the core lawmaking functions of the House. And lawmaking is not simply a matter of drafting and passing laws. Rather, it is a complex process that blends three interlocking elements: *representation*, *deliberation*, and *public education.*

The House's Basic Tasks

As reflected in its name, the House of Representatives is intended to be the branch of national government most responsive to the public will. As James Madison explained, the House should have "an immediate dependence upon, and an intimate sympathy with, the people."[1] Members are elected directly by the people every two years, to ensure that they do not stray very far from popular opinion. For most members, this two-year cycle means nonstop campaigning, visiting, errand running, and looking after constituents. Although senators, especially those from smaller states,[2] have taken on more of these same activities since the Seventeenth Amendment was ratified (in 1913), representatives perform them as a constitutional mandate and a political imperative.

While representing their constituents, members of the House are expected to deliberate among themselves as they examine public issues and craft legislative remedies. To help ensure sound decisionmaking, the Founders fashioned electoral mechanisms to promote the selection of qualified leaders and envisioned an institutional environment that would encourage genuine deliberation.[3] In practice, deliberation embraces, among other things, such basic interpersonal processes as problem solving, bargaining, persuasion, and leadership.[4] In the House, an elaborate committee system with jealously guarded jurisdictional boundaries has historically supplied the main arenas where problem solving and bargaining take place. In the chamber, stringent rules, as well as procedures designed to protect majority-party agendas and manage congested calendars, have worked to constrict the quality of debate and its influence upon members and the general public.[5] Thus, unlike their Senate colleagues, representatives now enjoy relatively limited opportunities for engaging in protracted debate.[6] Deliberation in the House therefore takes place mainly offstage—in committees, among the leadership, within informal task forces, and in the corridors—where members need not worry that their constituents or C-SPAN viewers are watching.[7]

Public understanding of the work of Congress flows not only from the conduct of representation and deliberation, but also from the way that these processes are communicated to constituents, elites, and the general public. Although few people outside the Beltway need to master the intricacies of parliamentary procedure, the public benefits from a rough understanding of how laws are made. Long-term public support, moreover, hinges upon an underlying feeling that legislators are capable, responsive, and ethical; that procedures permit the expression of a wide range of relevant viewpoints, including their own; that the institution is nonetheless not in the thrall of well-heeled "special interests"; and that the institution as a whole is capable of producing results in the form of laws that command widespread acceptance and compliance.

Because of the House's unique character, its optimal mix of attributes necessarily differs from those of the Senate. Among these elements are the following: First, the House is a comparatively large legislative entity: its 435 members (plus five nonvoting members) and more than 11,000 staff aides constitute a sizable working community. Second, the House is a complex enterprise, embracing a large number of work groups: committees, subcommittees, task forces, and informal caucuses and groups. Third, in processing legislation the House relies upon an elaborate division of labor through committee specialization. Fourth, the House's scheduling and deliberation are managed hierarchically through party leadership. In contrast with the Senate, therefore, a smoothly functioning House of Representatives would feature strong party and committee leadership, even at the expense of individual members' participation and influence. Deliberation in more manageably sized work groups—primarily committees, but also other bodies, such as task forces—more often than not takes precedence over debate in the full chamber.

In Search of Specific Measures of Institutional Health

Like the sport of baseball, the U.S. Congress has attracted collectors and devotees of statistics. The large number of legislators, and their collective activities—such as sponsoring legislation, attending committee and floor debates, casting votes, and offering amendments—has made irresistible the compiling of lists and statistics of all types. This advantage has attracted quantitatively oriented political observers, who have spawned an enormous and growing body of literature. Mainly because of its larger size and greater computational possibilities, the House enjoys an advantage over the Senate and therefore attracts substantially more attention from scholars. (Chamber size, however, has precisely the opposite effect on public and media attention.)

Indicators of all kinds are computed not only by scholars, but by representatives themselves, by officers of the chamber, by support agencies such as the Congressional Research Service and the Congressional Budget Office, by journalists and pundits, and by all sorts of lobby groups. Much material appears in the public record or is derived from it. Political scientists Norman J. Ornstein, Thomas E. Mann, and Michael J. Malbin have since the late 1970s published a biennial compendium of indicators.[8] Their volumes are a starting point for scholars, journalists, and interested observers seeking information about Congress. Some, though by no means all, of these data would be grist for the evaluative mills. Another key source is Congressional Quarterly, whose specialized publications—CQ Weekly,

CQ Almanacs, and special reports—have been issued steadily since the late 1940s. CQ pioneered in compiling annual floor voting studies, an example now followed by *National Journal* and many scholars and lobby organizations (Americans for Democratic Action and the American Conservative Union lay down, respectively, liberal and conservative benchmarks). Data on members' staffs and offices are periodically compiled and analyzed by the Congressional Management Foundation, a nonpartisan group devoted to improving organization and management in offices on both sides of Capitol Hill.[9]

Many studies by individual scholars illuminate aspects of congressional performance, although their data are all too rarely extended beyond the time periods of their initial research projects. A conspicuous exception is the index of ideological floor voting compiled by Keith T. Poole and Howard Rosenthal.[10] Another ambitious enterprise is the compilation of congressional historical statistics undertaken by Elaine K. Swift and her colleagues, and available as computer files through the Interuniversity Consortium for Political and Social Research.[11]

Inasmuch as the House's core functions—representation, deliberation, and public education—are expansive, we need to seek out specific measures, or indicators, of institutional health and effectiveness.[12] Some are *input variables* or attributes. What resources does the House command—in personnel, facilities, legal prerogatives, and the like—that enable it to perform its prescribed functions? Others are *process variables*. What practices and procedures are available as the House performs its duties? What are their effects on representation, deliberation, and public education? Still others are *output variables*. What are the products generated by the institution? What qualities do these products display—for example, in terms of quantity, quality, specificity, comprehensiveness, and credibility? Finally, there are what might be called *outcome variables*. What are the social, economic, and cultural effects of the House's actions? Inasmuch as these last-mentioned effects often become manifest only after the passage of time—take, for example, the impact of the land-grant college system or the G.I. Bill of Rights or the food-stamp program—we may need to search for provisional or surrogate measures of long-term significance. Students have shown great ingenuity in devising ways to identify significant legislative actions, whether historically or contemporaneously.[13] An important part of the House's evaluation would certainly be whether, and how, it dealt with those issues deemed most important by its own leaders, by the specialized press, and by attentive publics.[14]

For individual members, such measures might include: the quality and diversity of members' backgrounds, the balance between senior members and newcomers, and agreed-upon standards of personal performance and ethical behavior. For the institution and its operations, key factors would include: predictable scheduling, experienced leaders of work groups with clear jurisdictional mandates, adequate staff assistance, a compatible physical environment, clear and understandable rules and precedents, and a balance between strong leadership and channels for member participation. The House's levels of productivity and interpersonal comity also deserve public judgment, in spite of the prevalence of personal and partisan ambitions. Such output variables are more easily counted than interpreted. But within limits, the discrete products of the deliberative process—bills and resolutions, hearings, reports, oversight efforts, timely authorizations and appropriations, and legislation addressing pressing public issues—can tell us a great deal about the work and effectiveness of the House.

Public understanding and acceptance of the institution might be manifested in such measures as the level of public interest in the House and its operations, the number of Capitol Hill visitors, citizens' communications with members, and C-SPAN viewership. Mass assessments of the House and its members, as revealed, for example, in public opinion surveys and reelection rates, are important but distressingly imperfect measures of the institution's bonds with its publics.

Such measurements must be viewed in terms of their relevance to the fundamental functions of the House: representation, deliberation, and public understanding. Because of the House's unique characteristics—its large size, among other things—its optimal mix of attributes will necessarily differ from that of the Senate. More weight must be given to strong party and committee leadership at the expense of individual members' participation and influence. Deliberation in more manageably sized work groups—primarily committees but also other bodies, such as task forces and informal caucuses—will normally take precedence over debate in the chamber.

Suggested specific indicators are discussed below and summarized in appendix A. While not exhaustive, this list is intended to suggest the kinds of information that could form the ingredients of periodic reports on the institutional attributes of the House.

Representation

The recruitment and retention of qualified members is a necessary condition for an effective institution, whatever its size and purpose may be.

Although there seems to be no shortage of willing contenders for House seats, some commentators have worried that the "best and brightest" potential candidates all too often refuse to put their names forward or shun political life altogether. Typically, we gauge this by the number of nonincumbent candidates in congressional races who are deemed "quality" contenders—that is, individuals with obvious political assets, such as previous public officeholding or other notable service in the community or state.[15] Thus it is troubling that such a potential candidate as Claudia Kennedy, the highest ranking woman ever to serve in the U.S. Army when she retired in 2000, declined after an exploratory campaign to challenge four-term incumbent Republican senator John Warner. A spokeswoman said Ms. Kennedy lacked enthusiasm for the nonstop fund-raising and campaign schedule that would have been required: "She would have to spend almost all of her campaign time raising money, and that is not the way she wants to campaign."[16]

Congressional elections are, of course, profoundly affected by who runs and who declines to run for office. A key element in everyone's electoral calculus is "incumbent advantage": the greater visibility, reputation, and resources enjoyed by sitting members than by virtually all of their challengers. Awareness of this advantage no doubt dissuades many potential contenders from throwing their hats into the ring. Unless they have personal wealth, those who do take the plunge face the daunting task of raising enough money to wage a credible campaign. Little wonder, then, that parties and individual contenders focus on a small number of open seats, and that many incumbents coast to reelection without serious opposition.

Important as the questions of candidate recruitment and campaign finance are, they depend only tangentially upon the quality of the House as a workplace. Moreover, some elements, such as those relating to recruitment and candidate emergence, are exceedingly difficult to conceptualize and measure. Our project investigators have therefore decided to focus on measurements of the institutions' organizational and policymaking capacities.

Extent and Diversity of Members' Backgrounds

The House has never been a microcosm of American society. By almost any measure, its members constitute an economic and social elite. They are overwhelmingly white and male; they are well educated and tend to come from a small number of prestigious professions, mainly law and business. Must the members demographically mirror the populace to perform their representational tasks? Probably not. But members' backgrounds affect their legislative priorities; conversely, underrepresented and unrepresented groups feel, probably rightly, that their interests are likely to be overlooked.

Thus an inventory of members' characteristics and backgrounds is one element in any well-rounded inventory of a given Congress. Among the data to be collected would be the following: percent of representatives from various occupations and professions; those with previous government experience; those who have served in municipal, county, and state offices; information on age, race, gender, and religious affiliation; educational attainment and economic status. Most of these data are readily available.

Member Turnover

What constitutes an optimal member turnover level is far from obvious. The House clearly requires a mixture of seasoned veterans and lively newcomers. But what mixture would be ideal? Some periods are marked by a dramatic "changing of the guard"; in others few incumbents retire or are defeated. On average, about 15 percent of newly elected House members are freshmen. However, turnover rates over the 1953–99 period fluctuated from a low of 8 percent to a high of 25 percent.[17] As a compromise, one might report numerically how turnover in any given year deviates from the long-term mean. In 1993, for example, the turnover rate was +10 after hordes of incumbents departed in the wake of the "House Bank" scandal. In 2000, a low turnover year, the index was –6. Such a simple index would place a current event or recent trend in chronological perspective. Similarly, the mean terms of House members would tap the same institutional attribute, even though the numbers shift relatively little. During the modern period (1953–2003), the mean seniority of the House has been 5.2 terms, or a little more than ten years.[18] In the wake of high turnover in the early 1990s, mean seniority of the three most recent Congresses dropped somewhat below normal. This followed an unusually high mean seniority in the 1987–93 period (the 100th through 102d Congresses).

Among the variables that should be monitored, then, are the following: mean tenure of representatives; mean election and reelection margins; mean turnover in previous elections; proportion of first termers; and distribution by seniority.

Whether voluntary or not, retirement—"de-recruitment," as Stephen E. Frantzich once termed it—is an important if neglected aspect of the

House's personnel picture.[19] It would be useful to monitor retirees' personal attributes (such as age, seniority, party, ideology, electoral margins). Moreover, there should be systematic exit interviews with members that would include not only the individual's reasons for leaving—such as electoral problems (defeat, vulnerability, redistricting, scandal), health, family or business considerations, or dissatisfaction with the House—but would also probe the retiree's experiences and assessments of the House and its operations. (Although it does not conduct exit interviews as such, the Senate Historian's Office has compiled a valuable series of oral history interviews with former senators and staff members.) Such interviews would also help to clarify the House's organizational strengths and weaknesses. "Studying [the] replacement process," Frantzich explains, "helps us to understand where we have been, where we are going, and what instigated the process of change."[20]

Deliberation

The process of deliberation involves several related activities: position taking, discussion, problem solving, debating, bargaining, and conflict resolution. To the extent that the House succeeds as a lawmaking body, it must encourage its members to use all these techniques in addressing public questions. Given the House's size and complexity, there must be mechanisms for scheduling and organizing different forms of deliberation in committee rooms, on the floor, and elsewhere.

Scheduling

For the average representative, allocating time requires exceedingly tough personal and political choices. Capitol Hill duties must be balanced against repeated trips to the district. On the Hill, legislative duties must be performed along with constituency and political chores.

As for members' families, whether they reside in Washington or in the representative's home district, they too pay a high price exacted by the demands of holding public office. In two focus groups convened in July 2000, members and their spouses described in detail the financial burdens of maintaining two households and the strain of separation while members spend long hours on legislative business and campaign for reelection. "This is a very tough business on family," observed House GOP Conference chair J. C. Watts (R-Okla.) in 2001. "You miss a lot of Little League, a lot of dance recitals."[21] Watts again cited family concerns when announcing his retirement from the House the following year. Another 2002 retiree, Sen. Fred Thompson (R-Tenn.), noted that in Congress, "Your schedule is not your own."[22]

Many of these scheduling conflicts are inevitable, but the issue warrants closer inspection than it has received. An inventory of indicators would include the following: (1) weekly and daily committee and floor schedules; (2) reliability of the House's schedules; (3) balance between committee and floor work; (4) time budgets for a sample of members; (5) compatibility of work schedules with family and personal obligations. Members' fund-raising needs also affect their time budgets: time spent fund-raising affects the ease of scheduling House committee and floor business and may impair the ability of members to interact with each other and to participate in the collective work of the House.

Our impression of members' work schedules—that they are long, demanding, hectic, and fragmented—probably captures the essence of congressional workdays, but it is based on scattered observations and anecdotal evidence. Despite the importance of scheduling in members' priorities—nearly 84 percent of House members questioned by the 1993 Joint Committee felt strongly that scheduling should be a target for reorganization[23]—neither congressional agencies nor outside researchers have succeeded in compiling a detailed record of members' daily time budgets. No one, to my knowledge, has been able to replicate the 1969 study of 158 members that described a typical 59.3-hour workweek.[24] Despite the obvious difficulties, such an inventory should be undertaken at least once a decade.

Quality of Committee Deliberations

The quality of House policymaking depends to a great degree on the quality of its committee deliberations. House reformers of recent decades have accordingly focused on the committee system. They have tried to reduce committee sizes and assignments, rationalize committee jurisdictions, improve scheduling, and enhance the quality and availability of staffs. The last comprehensive committee reorganization—much compromised by entrenched committee leaders—occurred in 1975.[25]

When Republicans captured the House twenty years later, their leaders initially contemplated sweeping jurisdictional changes. It turned out, however, that GOP chairs-to-be were just as jealous of their prerogatives as the Democrats they had replaced. So jurisdictional adjustments were minimal, although three minor committees (all with predominantly Demo-cratic clienteles) were eliminated.[26]

Standing committee jurisdictions are therefore often outdated and in-flexible in comparison with today's complex, interlocked policy questions. Evolving policy challenges rarely fit neatly into the jurisdictional catego-ries that were codified years or even decades ago. Increasingly, the com-mittees are supplemented or even supplanted by alternative organizational entities: multicommittee arrangements, partisan or bipartisan task forces, leadership-convened panels, outside blue-ribbon commissions, and high-level "summit" conferences between legislative leaders and the executive branch. The House's future challenge will be to combine the traditional virtues of committee expertise with the need for flexible responses to broad policy issues.

For representatives to concentrate on committee deliberations, as they should in the House in order to maximize their influence, they need suffi-cient time and resources. Procedural changes introduced by the GOP in 1995 were aimed at focusing members' attention on their committee du-ties, but these have failed to resolve some of the underlying problems of the committee system.

For one thing, House committees remain excessively large (see table 2-1). House Transportation and Infrastructure is, with seventy-four mem-bers, the largest committee on Capitol Hill; House Appropriations has sixty-five members and works mainly through its thirteen subcommittees. Other major committees are also large: the House's thirteen primary policymaking committees average almost fifty-three members apiece, and the numbers have gone up, not down, since the Republican takeover in 1995. And because the House has tried to limit the number of subcom-mittees, many of these panels are also sizable. Such work groups have grown too large for real deliberation by their members; indeed, few com-mittee rooms can comfortably accommodate them.

Committee effectiveness in the House is affected also by the number of assignments held by individual members. The average representative holds seats on almost six committees and subcommittees (see table 2-1). In the 1990s, both before and after the Republicans retook control of the House, several committees were eliminated and member assignments diminished. But members are still overcommitted in their committee assignments. This is a difficult problem for the party leaders who influence the assignments: their members clamor for assignments that will help them get reelected, and how can party leaders resist such appeals?

Table 2-1. *House Committee Statistics, 1991–2002*

Item	Congress					
	102d (1991–92)	103d (1992–94)	104th (1995–96)	105th (1997–98)	106th (1999–2000)	107th (2001–02)
Number of committees	27	23	20	20	20	20
Number of subcommittees	149	117	86	92	87	93
Mean committee size	37.9	38.6	39.2	40.1	41.7	42.4
Maximum committee size	68	62	62	73	75	74
Mean number of assignments	7	5.9	4.8	5.0	5.1	5.8

Sources: Author's calculations from *Congressional Quarterly*: "The 102nd Congress: A Committee Directory," May 4, 1991; "Players, Politics and Turf of the 103rd Congress," May 1, 1993; "Players, Politics and Turf of the 104th Congress," March 25, 1995; "Players, Politics and Turf of the 105th Congress," March 22, 1997; and "The Hill People 1999," *National Journal*, June 19, 1999; *Congressional Directory 2001–2002* (Government Printing Office, 2001), pp. 387–442.

Committee work is also affected by the presence of competing policy centers within the House. Among the competitors to committees are leadership-controlled committees (for example, Budget and Rules), partisan task forces, and interbranch "summit conferences." There is every reason to believe that House committees have increasingly been bypassed in favor of such alternative forums.[27] The question is whether the rise of these alternative mechanisms for policy development has constricted members' commitment to, and time for, the details of committee work.

Among the measures relevant to committee deliberations, the following are illustrative rather than exhaustive: (1) size and organization of committees; (2) numbers of members' committee and subcommittee assignments; (3) representativeness of committee membership; (4) members' participation rates in committee hearings, markups, and votes; (5) jurisdictional clarity; multicommittee handling of subject matter; (6) committee leadership and staffing; (7) committee productivity, including number of hearings and meetings, legislative versus oversight hearings, and legislative and other reports; (8) committee-leadership relationships, which have been flashpoints especially since Newt Gingrich held the speakership; (9) the overall size and scope of committees' agendas; and (10) the disposition or impact of committee products. Given variations in committee jurisdictions, the focus may be less on the absolute workload levels than on the eventual fate of committee efforts.

Quality of Floor Deliberation and Debate

Among the variables that might be ingredients in evaluating floor deliberations are: (1) the scheduling of floor sessions: legislation and other business; (2) special rules: open versus closed, time limits, and other features; (3) amendments: number and significance; (4) the resolution of differences and voting; (5) the tone of debates, including the level of interpersonal comity.

Analysis of House floor voting, long a staple of scholarly and interest group studies, can help us understand the kinds of choices faced by lawmakers. Floor votes are, of course, only the tip of the legislative iceberg: in the House especially, votes are often structured (especially under special rules) to offer limited alternatives and even to yield results desired by the leadership. So voting data must be approached with care. Nonetheless, voting statistics can reveal the extent of partisanship, the level of "gridlock," the impact of various political forces, and even the effectiveness of party and committee leadership.

Partisan differences over policy goals and means are manifest in voting records. Party affiliation is the strongest single correlate of members' voting decisions, and in recent years party-line voting has reached surprisingly high levels. However, patterns of party division are varied: there is *partisanship* (voting strictly according to party membership), *bipartisanship* (consensus voting), and *cross-partisanship* (nonparty voting).[28] The much-noted rise of partisan voting does not necessarily mean the demise of bipartisan or even cross-partisan voting. However, partisan polarization seems to increase the likelihood of stalemate on important legislative issues;[29] accordingly, another element of partisanship worth calculating is the number of political moderates.[30]

Bicameral Relations

House workways embrace also the conditions for reaching bicameral agreement. Gridlock is more likely when the House and Senate prefer significantly different versions of a bill or disagree on whether there should be legislation at all. In evaluating the workways of the House, attention must be paid to the state of bicameral relations and negotiations.

Among the indicators worth examining are: (1) the frequency of interchamber communications among leaders, committees, members, and staffs; (2) the use of formal mechanisms for reaching interhouse agreement, including conference committees; (3) the timeliness and final disposition of House-Senate disputes; and (4) adherence to House rules and conference committee precedents concerning interchamber negotiations.

Staff Support

STAFF SIZE: PERSONAL, COMMITTEE, CHAMBER, SUPPORT AGENCIES. More than 11,000 people are employed by the House of Representatives, in members' offices, committees, leadership offices, and the chamber itself (see table 2-2.) Since the 1980s, following a long period of growth, this figure has leveled off; in fact, House staffs have been reduced about 13 percent since the advent of Republican control in 1995. Committee staff cuts have been especially harsh: on average, committee staffs in four recent Congresses (1995–2001) were some 40 percent below the average during Democratic Congresses (1979–94). Chamberwide staffs were cut by more than one-fourth. In contrast, members' personal staffs have declined hardly at all, and leadership staffs have expanded slightly.

Appropriations for congressional operations have increased dramatically in the modern era. Reformers and critics of the mid-twentieth century found Congress seriously understaffed and unequipped to cope with executive-branch expertise. One of the hallmarks of the so-called reform era (roughly, the late 1960s through the mid-1970s), therefore, was improved staffing and facilities for members, committees, and support agencies. The Congressional Budget Office (CBO) and the Office of Technology Assessment (OTA) were launched; major expansions were authorized for the Congressional Research Service (CRS) and the General Accounting Office (GAO). After 1976, as the reform era was winding down, House expenditures stabilized. Since then, the figures have lagged behind cost-of-living indexes.[31]

Support agencies' personnel have been cut, in some cases drastically, since 1995. Largely on the House's initiative, OTA was eliminated that year. The General Accounting Office was downsized by almost 30 percent, reportedly because Republican leaders judged the agency's oversight activities to be overly aggressive and biased in favor of Democratic leaders' project requests. (In fairness to GAO, one must understand that its oversight work for Congress results primarily from committee requests. This meant, at least before 1995, that Democratic committee and subcommittee leaders originated a large proportion of the requests for investigations. GOP-controlled Congresses, however, have presumably received favorable treatment.) Another congressional research arm, CRS, faced staff

Table 2-2.   *House and Support Agency Staffing Levels, 1979–2001*

Staff or agency[a]	1979–94 Democratic control (8 Congresses)	1995–2001 Republican control (4 Congresses)	Change	
			Number	Percentage
House of Representatives				
Committee staff	2,129	1,253	–876	–40.3
Personal staff	7,440	7,223	–217	–1.5
Chamber staff	1,673	1,236	–437	–26.1
Leadership staff	140	146	+6	+4.1
Total staff	11,382	9,858	–1,524	–13.4
Support agencies				
Congressional Budget Office	221	227	+6	+2.7
Congressional Research Service	849	724	–125	–14.7
General Accounting Office	5,072	3,568	–1,504	–29.7
Office of Technology Assessment[b]	140	. . .	–140	–100.0
Total support staff	6,282	4,519	–1,763	–28.1

Source: Norman J. Ornstein, Thomas E. Mann, and Michael J. Malbin, *Vital Statistics on Congress 2001–2002* (American Enterprise Institute Press, 2002), pp. 126–27, 134.

a. House mean staff figures are based on biennial counts (odd-numbered years); mean support agency staff figures are based on annual counts.

b. The Office of Technology Assessment (OTA) was phased out in 1995.

cuts of nearly 15 percent. Among the support agencies, only CBO escaped downsizing.

Are the House's staffing and allowances adequate for the tasks that are demanded of it? That is not an easy question to answer; surveys of members and staffs, plus spot checks of office operations, would help to clarify the situation. Concern centers on those committees that absorbed especially severe staff cutbacks (for example, Appropriations, Banking, Commerce, Education and the Workforce, and Ways and Means). Equally problematic are the drastic cuts sustained by CRS and especially GAO, agencies charged with assisting members and committees in laying out policy alternatives (CRS) and examining exeuctive-agency activities (GAO). No matter which party controls Congress, or what its agenda, these functions are essential to lawmaking.

Members' offices, of course, have retained their staffing levels since at least the early 1980s. These offices always seem crowded and overburdened, but the leveling off of staffs (averaging 14.2 full-time aides per member in 1998) has been at least partially offset by computerization and extensive use of volunteers (averaging eight interns and 0.4 fellows per year per office). Crowding in Capitol Hill offices has been further alleviated by the fact that 44 percent of members' aides are now deployed in district offices.[32]

STAFF COMPENSATION AND TURNOVER.   The House has not one staff but many staffs. The various categories of offices—chamber, leadership, committee, and individual member—tend to operate and recruit independently, although there is some mobility from office to office. The average House staffer is young, well educated, single, and without children. Professional jobs in the chamber and in the committees tend to be marked by more stability and relatively generous compensation. Member staffs, whether in the districts or on Capitol Hill, tend to be characterized by lower pay and higher turnover. The Congressional Management Foundation (CMF) periodically tracks House and Senate staff conditions, using salary and interview data. CMF's most recent study of House employees highlighted continuing problems of short job tenure and high turnover. Pay gaps were found between Hill employees and federal government employees, between senior House employees and their Senate counterparts, and among gender, racial, and ethnic categories.[33] CMF Executive Director Rick Shapiro, reflecting on one recent study, declared, "Congress has to raise the question: Are we prepared to lose increasing numbers of our staff, and what is the cost benefit to the institution."[34]

Periodic surveys such as those undertaken by CMF are valuable in assessing the work capacity of the House. They should be continued on a biennial basis and extended to other categories of House employees. In the future, staff surveys should embrace not only quantitative data on recruitment, tenure, and salaries, but also qualitative testimony about working conditions in general.

QUALIFICATIONS OF STAFF MEMBERS.   Impressionistic evidence suggests that the House has largely succeeded in attracting talented staff aides, ranging from experienced professionals in committee posts to the young and energetic college graduates who tend to gravitate to members' offices. Inventories of the backgrounds of professional staffs could be undertaken periodically, perhaps by supplementing staff directory information with survey findings. These same types of variables should be collected to clarify the role and effectiveness of the congressional support agencies: the General

Accounting Office (GAO), the Congressional Research Service (CRS), and the Congressional Budget Office (CBO).

Public Education and Understanding

Insofar as possible, the deliberations and legislative output of the House should be readily available to all citizens. In combination with technological advances—primarily the Internet—the leadership and the Office of the Clerk have established a Legislative Resource Center and insisted that most documents (bill texts, hearing transcripts, reports, and other documents) be available online. Explanations of House rules, procedures, and practices (including relevant CRS reports concerning the legislative process) can be accessed through the House Rules Committee's website. Controversy has surrounded the public release of all CRS reports now generally available on Capitol Hill in hard copy or electronic form; however, it seems likely that these too will eventually be made available through the Internet. Any ongoing evaluation of the House's performance should include the monitoring of these services.

Communications with the Public

Constituent and public communications are leading tasks of members' offices. Overall statistics concerning these activities are either unavailable or difficult to obtain. As part of an evaluation of the work of the House and its members in this area, it would be useful to undertake periodic audits and spot checks of members' communications with constituents—including use of mail, the Internet, and radio and television—for purposes of information, outreach, and constituency service.

As for the House's public visage, this is for the most part a product of media coverage, including C-SPAN transmissions of floor proceedings. Unlike the Senate, the House as an entity makes little effort to explain itself and its work to the general public. No doubt this reticence reflects a justifiable fear that efforts at self-promotion would meet with skepticism from the press and the public. Yet the absence of serious journalistic coverage of institutional questions leaves the House even more vulnerable to negative and often inaccurate media caricatures of its work. Stephen Hess has gone so far as to propose that each chamber establish an Institutional Communications Office, whose mandate would be "to collect and provide nonpartisan information on the operations of Congress, including important events in congressional history, statistics and precedents, and historical comparisons."[35] "Because institutional reporting does not come comfortably to mainstream American press," Hess argues, "Congress must be better prepared to help explain—and defend—itself."[36]

Indeed, a large number of legislative bodies—ranging, in my personal observation, from the Australian National Assembly to the Washington State legislature—have successfully published pamphlets and other materials that explain their structures and procedures. In addition to distributing brochures to chamber visitors, the U.S. Senate publishes a unified series of nearly twenty pamphlets with online versions. The Senate's Historical Office, which was established in 1975 and enjoys bipartisan support, successfully performs numerous informational duties and provides current senators and staffs with a measure of institutional memory.

After hiring its first professional historian in 1983 to oversee the chamber's bicentennial observances, the House in 1989 created its own Office of the Historian. Never as generously supported as its Senate counterpart, however, the office was summarily abolished in 1995. Recently, the House has taken steps to restore the functions if not the outright title of this office. The House's performance on this score therefore deserves periodic oversight and evaluation.

Another aspect of public outreach, thus far sadly neglected, is the range and quality of services for the thousands of citizens who annually visit the Capitol. Before September 11, 2001, nearly 3 million people visited the Capitol, as many as 18,000 a day: "The numbers exceed the Capitol's capacity, as anyone who has waited in line can attest."[37] The construction of a Capitol Visitors' Center offers new opportunities for public education about how representatives go about the public's business. (Security concerns underscore the urgent need for such a center.) The new facilities will accommodate far more visitors than the current arrangements, and will enable them to enter the Capitol and visit House and Senate chambers in an orderly fashion. Visitors' facilities should extend beyond the obvious tourist amenities to displays and multimedia presentations that will illuminate the House and Senate as institutions.

Media Coverage

The levels of individual and institutional press coverage affect the public's perception of the House and its work. As noted already, this coverage varies over time, both quantitatively and qualitatively. Thus reviews of the House might well include periodic audits of the amount of coverage given the House and its members. The subjects of such coverage, and its positive or negative tone, would help us understand what people learn about the chamber.

Public Evaluations of the House and Its Members

In the public's eye, there are two Congresses, not just one: the citizen's own representative (or senator), who presents a representational image to the home folks; and the institution on Capitol Hill that engages in collective decisionmaking. People tend to see their own representatives as agents of local concerns. They measure their legislators by such yardsticks as service to the district, communication with constituents, and "home style"—the way the officeholder deals with home folks. In judging their representatives, voters tend to think in concrete terms: Do they trust the legislator? Does the legislator communicate well with the district? Does the legislator listen to the district and its concerns?[38]

The results of such perceptions are predictable. Individual members tend to be given high marks by their constituents. If voters think that elected officials as a class are untrustworthy scoundrels, they do not usually feel that way about their own representatives. Nor do they show sustained eagerness to "throw the rascals out." Since the mid-twentieth century, no less than 92 percent of the representatives who run for reelection have been successful.[39] Do these numbers reflect on institutional strengths or weaknesses? Perhaps, but only in a tangential way.

Surveys that probe the reasons for the public's ranking of individual members are less frequent than we would prefer. The general findings are, however, quite clear. When asked whether they approve of the way "your member of Congress" handles his or her job, citizens' ratings range some 20 to 30 percent higher than ratings of Congress as an institution, rarely falling to the level of 50 percent.[40]

Despite the obvious disparities in the levels of support, public ratings of individual members tend to follow the patterns of institutional approval and disapproval, rising in times of national optimism, sinking in times of doubt and scandal. There is evidence, moreover, that citizens' impressions of the fairness of Capitol Hill business—whether for example, procedures are open to everyone or are controlled by special interests—link levels of public approval of Congress *and* of their own representatives.[41]

Institutional Levels of Approval or Trust

Over the twenty-five-year period 1974–99, Congress's average approval rate (surveys rarely distinguish between the two chambers) has been 40.6

percent; disapproval has been 59.4 percent—dichotomizing the responses and eliminating those expressing no opinion.[42] Only rarely have the public's estimations of Congress been positive overall: for example, during the immediate post-Watergate period (1974); during the economic recovery of the mid-1980s (1985–87); early in the George H. W. Bush administration (1989); after the Persian Gulf war (1991); in the pre-impeachment phase of Clinton's second term (1998); and in the post-9/11 period. Current rankings could be evaluated in terms of their deviation from the long-term mean. A recent fairly positive rating of 49 percent, for example, could be seen as eight points above the twenty-five-year average, or +8—a respectable level of support, even though a slight majority of those respondents who held opinions expressed a negative view.

The House versus Other Governmental Entities

According to the few surveys that have addressed the subject, people expect Congress to exert a vigorous, independent role in addressing public policy questions.[43] They want Congress to counterbalance the president's leadership, even in foreign policy matters. This seems to mean that citizens normally acquiesce in the notion of divided government, so that the two branches can keep a watchful eye upon each other. Although these findings have remained surprisingly consistent over the years, the surveys themselves are infrequent; moreover, they do not distinguish between the House and Senate. One element of a comprehensive plan to monitor public attitudes toward the House would be to increase the frequency and specificity of such surveys.

Another measure of interbranch relations would be a qualitative assessment of the House's success in articulating and defending its constitutional prerogatives. In the wake of the Iran-contra scandal, Louis Fisher, a leading scholar of separation of powers, pointed out:

> Executive dominance in foreign affairs is not healthy for Congress, the country, or even the president. . . . Shortcuts seem attractive; officials can circumvent laws with what they think are clever interpretations. Political appointees can initiate actions that injure Congress, the president, and the political system. They may be so eager for results, and so ignorant of constitutional processes, that they seek immediate payoffs despite long-term damage. The task of cleaning up the debris is left to careerists and professionals in Congress and the executive branch.[44]

Tensions between congressional leaders and President George W. Bush over access to government intelligence information on terrorism reminded us once again that the president's duty as commander-in-chief and Congress's mandate to authorize conflict and provide for armed forces can easily lead to competing claims over intelligence, especially during armed conflicts.[45] The House's record in asserting and shouldering its institutional duties under the Constitution has been notably inconsistent and is worth monitoring by unbiased experts.

Specialized Measures

Other dimensions of the public's attitudes toward the House and its members can be probed. There have been numerous surveys of such items as trust in public officials, the ethical standards of members, the influence of campaign money and lobbying, and the level of members' empathy with constituents. Not all these items appear consistently in surveys. However, several of these lines of questioning could provide valuable feedback if employed regularly.[46]

Summary

In this essay I have tried to suggest ways of establishing periodic, systematic institutional evaluations of our national government entities, in this case the House of Representatives. For a variety of reasons, evaluations of the House's health and effectiveness are rarely forthcoming from those who observe or comment about the House, much less from incumbent lawmakers. To provide the kind of evaluation not presently available, I have suggested the institutional checkup, a device that in one form or another has proved its value in a wide range of settings.

Implementing institutional evaluations as an ongoing enterprise will require considerable thought and planning. Intellectual and practical issues must be addressed and resolved. Among the questions to be answered are these: What independent, nonpartisan, and respected entity exists or could be created to undertake such a task? What data are already available to underpin such an analysis? What additional data would be essential or desirable, and how can those data be compiled? What role should be played by qualitative evidence, such as interviews with members and staffs, or judgments expressed by close observers of the House? How can these data be translated into understandable and meaningful categories? And how can these findings be disseminated so that different audiences—

reporters, scholars, activists, and the general public—can make substantive judgments about the quality of their national institutions of government?

Notes

1. Alexander Hamilton, James Madison, and John Jay, "Federalist No. 52," in *The Federalist Papers*, ed. Clinton Rossiter (Mentor, 1961), p. 327.

2. Frances E. Lee and Bruce I. Oppenheimer, *Sizing Up the Senate: The Unequal Consequences of Equal Representation* (University of Chicago Press, 1999).

3. Joseph M. Bessette, *The Mild Voice of Reason: Deliberative Democracy and American National Government* (University of Chicago Press, 1994).

4. Roger H. Davidson and Colton C. Campbell, "Deliberation in Congress: Past Traditions and Future Directions," paper presented at the annual convention of the American Political Science Association (Washington, D.C., 1997).

5. George E. Connor and Bruce I. Oppenheimer, "Deliberation: An Untimed Value in a Timed Game," in Lawrence C. Dodd and Bruce I. Oppenheimer, eds., *Congress Reconsidered*, 5th ed. (CQ Press, 1993).

6. Barbara Sinclair, *Unorthodox Lawmaking: New Legislative Processes in the U.S. Congress* (CQ Press, 1997).

7. C. Lawrence Evans and Walter J. Oleszek, *Congress under Fire: Reform Politics and the Republican Majority* (Houghton Mifflin, 1997).

8. A recent example is Norman J. Ornstein, Thomas E. Mann, and Michael J. Malbin, *Vital Statistics on Congress, 2001–2002* (American Enterprise Institute Press, 2002).

9. See, for example, Sheree L. Beverly, *1999 Senate Staff Employment Study* (Congressional Management Foundation, 1999); and *2000 House Staff Employment Study* (Washington, D.C.: Congressional Management Foundation, 2000).

10. Keith T. Poole and Howard Rosenthal, *Congress: A Political-Economic History of Roll Call Voting* (Oxford University Press, 1996).

11. Elaine K. Swift, Robert G. Brookshire, Evelyn C. Fink, John R. Hibbing, Brian D. Haines, Michael J. Malbin, and Kenneth C. Martis, *Database of Congressional Historical Statistics,* computer files (Ann Arbor, Mich.: Interuniversity Consortium for Political and Social Research, 2000).

12. William T. Gormley Jr. and David L. Weimer, *Organizational Report Cards* (Harvard University Press, 1999), pp. 61–75.

13. See, for example, Sarah A. Binder, "The Dynamics of Legislative Gridlock, 1947–1996," *American Political Science Review*, vol. 93 (September 1999), pp. 519–33.

14. Sarah A. Binder, "Does It Deliberate? Can It Act? Assessing the Institutional Health of the U.S. Senate," paper prepared for the Governance Institute's Workways of Governance Project (November 2001).

15. See, for example, Gary C. Jacobson and Samuel Kernell, *Strategy and Choice in Congressional Elections*, 2d ed. (Yale University Press, 1983).

16. John Mercurio, "Democrats Lose Another Top Recruit," *Roll Call*, September 27, 2001, p. 10.

17. Ornstein, Mann, and Malbin, *Vital Statistics*, pp. 16–17.

18. Ibid.

19. Stephen E. Frantzich, "De-Recruitment: The Other Side of the Congressional Equation," *Western Political Quarterly*, vol. 31 (March 1978), pp. 105–26.

20. Stephen E. Frantzich, "Opting Out: Retirement from the House of Representatives, 1966–1974," *American Politics Quarterly*, vol. 6 (July 1978), pp. 251–73.

21. Amy Keller, "The Life of a Lawmaker: Members, Wives Pour Out Hearts in Focus Groups," *Roll Call*, October 1, 2001, pp. 1, 13. .

22. Quoted in Mary Lynn F. Jones, "Family Concerns Prompt Early Hill Retirements," *Roll Call*, March 20, 2002, p. 12.

23. U.S. Congress, Joint Committee on the Organization of the Congress, Final Report, H. Rept. 103–413, 103 Cong. 1 sess. (Government Printing Office, 1993), vol. 2, p. 246.

24. Donald G. Tacheron and Morris K. Udall, *The Job of the Congressman*, 2d ed. (Bobbs-Merrill, 1970), pp. 303–11. The survey and its findings were originally analyzed in John S. Saloma, *Congress and the New Politics* (Boston: Little, Brown, 1969), pp. 183–95.

25. The effort is recounted in Roger H. Davidson and Walter J. Oleszek, *Congress against Itself* (Indiana University Press, 1977).

26. Evans and Oleszek, *Congress under Fire*, pp. 91–101.

27. Sinclair, *Unorthodox Lawmaking*, chap. 2.

28. Joseph Cooper and Garry Young, "Partisanship, Bipartisanship, and Crosspartisanship in Congress since the New Deal," in Lawrence C. Dodd and Bruce I. Oppenheimer, eds., *Congress Reconsidered*, 6th ed. (CQ Press, 1997), pp. 246–73.

29. Binder, "The Dynamics of Legislative Gridlock."

30. Sarah A. Binder, "The Disappearing Political Center," *Brookings Review*, vol. 15 (Fall 1996), pp. 36–39.

31. Ornstein, Mann, and Malbin, *Vital Statistics*, pp. 127, 140–41.

32. Beverly, *2000 House Staff Employment Study*, p. 50.

33. Ibid., pp. 1–2.

34. Quoted in "Senate Salaries Lag Behind," *Roll Call*, September 5, 2002, p. 1.

35. Stephen Hess, "The Decline and Fall of Congressional News," in Thomas E. Mann and Norman J. Ornstein, eds., *Congress, the Press, and the Public* (American Enterprise Institute / Brookings, 1994), p. 153.

36. Ibid., 152.

37. U.S. Capitol Historical Society, "The Capitol Visitor Center" (Fall 2001), p. 6.

38. Glenn R. Parker and Roger H. Davidson, "Why Do Americans Love Their Congressmen So Much More than Their Congress?" *Legislative Studies Quarterly*, vol. 4 (February 1979), pp. 53–61.

39. Roger H. Davidson and Walter J. Oleszek, *Congress and Its Members*, 8th ed. (CQ Press, 2000), pp. 63–65.

40. Ibid., pp. 426–28.

41. John R. Hibbing and Elizabeth Theiss-Morse, *Congress as Public Enemy* (Cambridge University Press, 1995).

42. Survey files archived in www.washingtonpost.com.

43. Diane Hollern Havey, "Who Should Govern? Public Preferences for Congressional and Presidential Power" (Ph.D. dissertation, University of Maryland, 1998).

44. Louis Fisher, *The Politics of Shared Power: Congress and the Executive* (CQ Press, 1993), p. 176.

45. Todd S. Purdum and Alison Mitchell, "Bush, Angered by Leaks, Duels with Congress," *New York Times*, October 10, 2001, pp. A1, B11.

46. See Hibbing and Theiss-Morse, *Congress as Public Enemy*.

THREE   *The Senate:*
Does It Deliberate?
Can It Act?

SARAH A. BINDER

"There is no quality of life in the Senate," observed
Warren Rudman (R-N.H.) several years after his 1992 retirement from
the U.S. Senate.[1] Reflecting on his experiences in the Senate, Rudman be-
moaned a chamber awash in partisanship and gridlock. For what they
suggest about the conditions of legislative life in the contemporary Senate, Rudman's observations about life in the Senate merit quoting at length:

> Why are outstanding people leaving who could serve in the Senate
> another decade or two? . . . Most [of the ones I've talked to] are
> leaving because the Senate has become so partisan, so frustrating,
> and so little fun. The number of votes that senators cast each year
> doubled between the 1960s and 1980s, and many of the extra votes
> are politically inspired and meaningless. Members serve on more
> committees . . . and cast more votes there. And it's not that more
> work means more results. More often it leads to posturing and par-
> tisan gridlock. . . . There's less time than ever for a social life or a
> family life, and the ever-increasing cost of running for election means
> that most senators must spend huge amounts of their time going
> with tin cup in hand to special interests for money.[2]

Rudman's portrait of the Senate hardly conjures up the image of a deliberative legislature and suggests that Senate working conditions have taken
their toll on its members and the health of the institution. A decade after
Rudman retired, there is little evidence that Senate life has improved, as

senators from both parties periodically lament the difficulties the Senate faces in trying to legislate.

In this chapter I consider the desirability and feasibility of evaluating the institutional health of the Senate, propose a theoretical framework and empirical approach for conducting such a checkup, and suggest a sample indicator that might routinely be used to evaluate the health of the Senate. Ultimately, the aim would be to craft a systematic exam that would be applied annually to monitor the conditions of governance in the upper legislative chamber.

The Feasibility and Desirability of an Institutional Checkup

Let me start by acknowledging the inevitable: The notion of devising a checkup for the Senate is fraught with difficulty. Conceptually, in devising a checkup we are crafting a means for periodically evaluating the institutional health and well-being of the Senate. Of course, when doctors conduct such an exam to rate people's physical health, it is based on a consensus of what constitutes a healthy human body. No such consensus exists for what constitutes a healthy legislative body, since such judgments are essentially normative calls about what makes a well-running political institution.

Why is it so difficult for political scientists (and others) to make such judgments? First and foremost is the problem of definition: What constitutes a good legislature? As Alan Rosenthal, an expert on state legislatures, has noted, "As far as good legislatures are concerned, like art, I can tell you what I like, but not exactly why. As far as bad legislatures are concerned, like pornography, I know them when I see them even though I cannot define what they are."[3] Even if appropriate criteria could be defined, it is doubtful that a consensus could be reached on which criteria are most important and thus deserve to be included in evaluating the institution's health. One major reason there would be such difficulty reaching a consensus lies in the nature of the endeavor. Unless we have some prior agreement on a *positive* assessment of legislatures, it is nearly impossible to make normative assessments. As Keith Krehbiel explains, in order to answer the question "'what is a good legislature?'" we have to first answer the question 'how do legislatures work?'"[4] Any perusal of the lengthy literature on legislative organization leads quickly to the following conclusion: There is little consensus on how legislatures work, which in turns compounds the difficulty of deciding how they *should* work.

Second, even if scholars or observers (or members!) of Congress could agree on a set of relevant criteria for what constitutes a good legislature, many of those criteria are likely to be mutually exclusive. Take, for example, a range of goals that Rosenthal sets for legislatures. Among them he includes the capacities for representativeness, responsiveness, and deliberation, noting that legislatures should have strong leadership, a dispersion of political power, and the capacity to address public problems.[5] Although such characteristics in isolation may resonate as desirable components of a good legislature, collectively the list of issues includes mutually exclusive goals. Can a legislature be both representative of diverse constituencies and responsive to public demands? Morris Fiorina's well-known study of Congress's difficulty in balancing those goals suggests not.[6] Can a legislature disperse political power and yet retain the capacity for deliberation and addressing problems? Steven S. Smith's analysis of the tensions among centralized, decentralized, and collegial institutions pointedly shows the difficulties of dispersing power and retaining decisionmaking capacity.[7] Thus, even if we could agree on a set of normative criteria by which to judge a legislature, conflicting criteria would make sweeping evaluations of the institution's health problematic.

Third, even if we could set standards and allow for trade-offs among them, it is not obvious that appropriate measures could ever be devised with which to rate legislative health. As Rosenthal acknowledges, some notions such as "deliberation, negotiation, and consensus building may be almost impossible to operationalize."[8] Compounding the problem of measurement is the concern that "the criteria that are easiest to measure are not necessarily the ones most important for a good legislature."[9] It may be relatively easy to count the number of staff assigned to legislators' personal offices, but it does not necessarily follow that large (or small) staffs are a critical gauge of a good legislature. And as Rosenthal worries, it may be that "what is most measurable is probably least significant and what is most significant is probably least measurable."[10]

Obstacles to devising an institutional checkup should raise flags about the feasibility of the endeavor. Should they also raise flags about the desirability of such an enterprise? I would argue that a checkup for the Senate is still desirable, although I fully recognize the inevitable pitfalls involved in creating and administering such a test to the patient. Thinking first about democratic expectations, there is ample reason to desire a review of Congress's institutional health. Quite simply, we live under a democratic system of representative government, one that was devised to ensure both the capacity for governance and the representation of interests. If Congress hesitates in meeting or pursuing either or both of those goals, representative government suffers. Because the health of representative government is also contingent on the public's ability to hold Congress accountable for its actions, educating the public about legislative process and performance is invaluable in facilitating such judgments. To be sure, citizens usually judge their own members' performance rather than Congress's collective performance at election time, but legislators' individual performance inevitably depends to some degree on the able functioning of Congress as an institution.[11]

Second, as Roger Davidson argues elsewhere in this volume, legislators have a limited incentive to focus on the health of the institution and even less incentive to share such assessments publicly. As David Mayhew forcefully argued in 1974, legislators' desire for reelection necessarily disinclines them to invest time, energy, and resources in institutional maintenance.[12] Even if we expand our notion of legislators' goals to include a broader mix of reelection, power, and policy motives, it is still not clear that members of either chamber would have much incentive to focus on institutional maintenance.[13] Given the lack of self-evaluation by the Congress, enlisting outsiders would be an invaluable step toward ensuring a serious effort to probe the health of the Senate.

Third, even if it is doubtful that we could reach consensus on the standards by which to judge a good legislature, there are still dividends to undertaking such an endeavor. Most simply, as argued by veteran state legislative scholar Malcolm Jewell, "A serious discussion of this issue may help us to understand legislatures better."[14] Even no less a positivist than Krehbiel argues that solid normative analysis may not be totally "hopeless," even if it is "necessarily premature" until positivists have done their own jobs better.[15] Institutional checkups are desirable, in other words, because the very process of devising them offers us the opportunity to refine our understanding of how legislatures work—a necessary precondition for eventually determining how they *should* work.

The Senate and the Problem of Collective Action

Acknowledging the hurdles bound to arise in devising a checkup for the Senate, I start by asking a simple question: What exactly do we expect of the Senate (and Congress more broadly) as a representative political institution? Once we identify the Senate's role, we can proceed to evaluate its ability to fulfill that role and thus its institutional health. In conducting an institutional checkup, we are essentially asking a two-part question: Under what conditions would the Senate best be able to pursue its designated role, and what evidence do we have that the Senate achieves or approaches that role? In evaluating the institutional health of the Senate, we should be attentive to matters of both *process* and *outcome*, two of the key criteria noted to be important in judging institutional health and efficiency more broadly.[16]

What role do we expect the Senate to perform? To answer this question, I start with two common claims about democratic government. First, at the heart of governmental action is the provision of public goods, and second, critical to the provision of public goods is collective action.[17] This is especially so in a legislature, where the development of policy expertise, durable coalitions, leadership strategies, and so on depends on the collective contributions of legislators endowed with equal voting rights under the Constitution. If collective action could be guaranteed, a legislature would arguably function seamlessly, as legislators would contribute in an equitable and judicious fashion to the smooth working of the institution and the careful provision of public goods.

In both theory and practice, however, collective action rarely occurs so seamlessly. Indeed, the provision of public goods is typically prone to a theoretical dilemma known as *the problem of collective action*: By acting rationally in what looks like their own self-interest, individuals may ultimately find themselves made worse off by their actions when public goods fail to be provided.[18] A typical example of a collective action problem is demonstrated by the annual fund-raising drives conducted by public radio stations. Assume that public radio is a public good because no one can be enjoined from listening to it and because one person's consumption of public radio does not diminish the supply. The problem of collective action suggests that it would not be rational for listeners to contribute money to public radio when they are solicited in an annual drive because they can consume the public good without contributing to its maintenance. Of course if *everyone* acted rationally, public radio could not be sustained and would go off the air; the public good would fail to be provided. That is why it is a good example of the problem of collective action: If everyone followed the individually rational decision not to contribute, everyone would be left worse off (when public radio goes off the air) than if they had chosen to contribute.[19] Acting rationally, in other words, may lead to inferior outcomes; cooperation, in contrast, may offer collective gains that outweigh the benefits of going it alone. The problem of collective action is thus a problem of coordination: How do you coordinate players' strategies to avert the collective action dilemma?

Overcoming problems of collective action inherent in the provision of public goods is arguably the central challenge for any legislative institution, and as I argue here, for the Senate in particular. There is good reason to suspect that the Senate may be frequently challenged by the problem of collective action, perhaps more so than the House. To be sure, both chambers have the constitutional duty to contribute to the creation, maintenance, and sometimes elimination of public goods. As such, both must be able to coordinate their members for collective action. In both chambers, legislators tend to rely on one of the traditional solutions for coordinating collective behavior: the creation of strong leadership. Although chamber and party leaders tend to have only limited tools for encouraging cooperative behavior, their leverage over the agenda, electoral resources, and institutional advancement is likely sufficient to compel the cooperation of many legislators much of the time. The point more generally is that voluntary agreements and good faith cannot reliably guarantee players' cooperation; some form of institutional enforcement is necessary.

The hitch for the Senate is that strong leadership is often in short supply. This is not a function of the types of leaders chosen, but of the weak procedural powers of the chamber's leaders. Numerous aspects of Senate rules and practices limit the procedural power of chamber and party leaders to coordinate the actions of their colleagues, at least in comparison with the powers afforded House leaders. Senate leaders need to secure cloture-proof majorities under Rule 22, often require unanimous consent on an ad hoc basis or in a complex time agreement, and have only limited ability to block unrelated (or "nongermane") amendments. Such weak procedural powers limit leaders' ability to compel or encourage collective action by 100 ambitious politicians.

Not only do leaders have to corral cooperation from their members; they also have to contend with competition between the two political parties. Disagreement between the two parties, for example, yielded stalemate in the 106th Congress (1999–2000) over tax cuts, education reform, minimum-wage increases, Medicare and Social Security reform, prescription drug coverage, managed health care reform, and gun control, to name just a few salient issues. How do you compel cooperation with the other party when there are strong partisan incentives to disagree? Senate leaders also need to coordinate bicameral agreement, a task complicated by senators' individual powers to stall the formation of conference committees and the consideration of conference agreements. In short, there is ample reason to suspect that the Senate, as well as the House, typically faces problems of collective action, but that the Senate may be procedurally more disadvantaged for that task than the House.

Components of an Institutional Checkup

Suppose then that the mark of a healthy legislature is its ability to coordinate its members into collective action. If so, we are defining Congress and the Senate's basic role as the ability to make decisions in response to pressing public problems. Decisionmaking capacity would thus be central in evaluating the institution's health. By placing decisionmaking capacity at the heart of an institutional checkup, a valid battery of tests would address matters of both process and outcome. With respect to process, we would want to monitor signs the Senate shows of being equipped to make legislative decisions. With respect to outcomes, we would want to set in place a device for monitoring the Senate's ability to reach policy decisions. As Malcolm Jewell nicely phrases it, "A legislature should be able to confront the major problems facing the state, rather than ignoring them."[20]

To evaluate the Senate's decisionmaking capacity, we need to identify the critical junctures of decisionmaking in the body and then devise indicators that would measure how well the Senate functions at those times. Here, I look at four stages of Senate decisionmaking: decisionmaking in committee, the setting of the floor agenda, decisionmaking on the Senate floor, and the bicameral negotiation of differences with the House. I conclude with a brief look at the "member-as-enterprise," exploring the strains senators and staff encounter in trying to handle the multiple and heavy demands of office.[21] For each stage, I consider when collective action problems are likely to arise and suggest potential indicators of the severity of those problems (see appendix B).

Committee Decisionmaking

Typically, far more attention is paid to committees in the House than in the Senate. As a larger body with fewer opportunities to amend bills on the floor, the House tends to rely far more heavily on its committees than does the Senate. Although senators, like House members, often develop policy expertise through their service on Senate panels, the combination of weak Senate limits on floor debate, the lack of a germaneness rule, and senators' larger state constituencies reduce their incentives to stake their legislative careers on committee service.[22]

Still, it would be a mistake to overlook committees in identifying obstacles to Senate decisionmaking because committees retain a central place in the crafting of policy alternatives and legislative bills for the chamber. For senators to cooperate in committee deliberations, they need the time and resources to do so. At issue is the ability of senators to meet the enormous set of demands they face daily. At the committee level, such demands are exacerbated by the number of committee and subcommittee assignments held and the resulting workload and competing time demands they generate, complaints voiced during hearings held in 1993 by the Joint Committee on the Organization of Congress.[23] As former senator David Boren reflected, "As I worked through my decision [to leave the Senate], I remembered 14-hour days: running from one room to another because four of my committees were meeting at the same time."[24]

The Stevenson reforms adopted in 1977 (named for Senator Adlai Stevenson, D.-Ill.) established strict limits on the number of committee and subcommittee assignments senators could hold. The Senate's ready willingness to waive these limits, however, is said to frequently undermine the intent of the Stevenson reforms.[25] As a result, senators often face time conflicts and unreasonable workload demands, which arguably harm committees' ability to convene hearings and markups and to attract the full attention and participation of their members. Although we lack more recent survey evidence probing senators' views, a survey by the Joint Committee on the Organization of Congress in 1993 found that three-quarters of Senate respondents (n = 25) favored additional limits on committee and subcommittee assignments.[26] Given such concerns about the impact of committee assignments, checkup indicators might monitor the number of committee and subcommittee assignments per senator and the number of waivers granted by the Senate each year.

Committee workloads might also be a source of collective action problems for chamber panels. Rudman's reflections quoted at the outset describe a committee system awash in votes, but not results. If committee efforts routinely end in gridlock or are ignored by the parent chamber, senators' incentives to invest time and energy at the committee level are surely diminished. The less willing senators are to invest their energies in committee work, the more likely collective action problems will arise at the committee level. Thus, in thinking about the impact of committee workloads, we should probably be less concerned about monitoring the size of workloads (say, time spent in session, numbers of bills considered, and so on) and more concerned about the eventual fate of committee efforts. A reasonable indicator of committee health would thus probe the percentage of salient agenda items that end in gridlock at the committee stage. To be sure, committees may deadlock because of genuine policy differences, an issue that raises the difficulty of interpreting scores of committee productivity.

Agenda Setting

Collective action problems can also occur at the stage of deciding which issues to put on the chamber's agenda. This is especially so in the Senate, where the majority leader has only limited control to determine the floor agenda for the chamber. Because issues are typically brought to the floor via a motion to proceed, the majority leader customarily needs either unanimous consent for the motion or a cloture-proof majority (required under Rule 22) should objections arise to the motion. The alternative, crafting a unanimous consent agreement, also limits the leader's ability to set the agenda because any single senator can threaten to object to the agreement or can place a hold on the measure. In either case, anywhere from narrow to complete bipartisanship may be required to set the Senate's agenda. Collective action problems are thus highly likely in setting the floor agenda because it entails the agreement of a supermajority of senators (usually sixty votes) or unanimous consent.

When differences between the two parties are especially pronounced, collective action problems are likely to emerge over the floor agenda. There are numerous examples of such conflict, including a series of impasses reached in the spring of 2000. Partisan differences over whether to allow a vote on gun control spilled over into a partisan tug-of-war over the rest of the majority party's agenda priorities.[27] Democrats retaliated against the Republicans' reluctance to hold votes on gun control by blocking consideration of annual spending bills that had yet to be passed by the House, derailing the majority party's control of the agenda.[28] "Holds" have also affected the Senate's ability to set its agenda, as senators from both parties have placed holds on bills and nominations either to block the measures single-handedly or to extract concessions on unrelated issues. Holds have been particularly effective in delaying consideration of executive and judicial branch nominations, including some that have languished despite significant bipartisan support for their confirmation. Although partisan and ideological differences make it difficult to determine just what a rational agenda-setting method should look like, the character of the process certainly affects the health of an institution and its decisionmaking capacity.

Several potential indicators for monitoring the agenda-setting capabilities of the Senate are possible. Such statistics might include the outcome, partisanship, and margins of victory on cloture votes as indicators of the level of conflict over the agenda. The frequency of complex time agreements and the length of time required to negotiate them might also indicate the Senate's ease of agenda setting. Indicators marking the frequency and resolution of holds would provide additional measures of the level of cooperation over the setting of the agenda.[29]

Floor Decisionmaking

Collective action problems are also likely to occur even after issues are successfully placed on the chamber's agenda for floor consideration. Because Senate rules require a supermajority to secure a vote in the face of minority opposition, coordinating the Senate to complete consideration of measures on the Senate floor can be a difficult enterprise. Disagreement over nongermane amendments offered during floor consideration may also spur extended debate and prevent the body from casting a final vote. We might also say that collective action problems occur when there are long delays in chamber deliberation, even if a final vote is eventually cast. Failure to obtain a chamber quorum because of absent senators or procedural motions designed to slow down the chamber might yield such delays. An example from a Senate staffer gives a flavor of the Senate's difficulties: "You could literally sit here all day long in an interminable Quorum call. Vote on it already. Do it. It just doesn't happen."[30]

Whatever the cause, chamber difficulty in managing its agenda would suggest that at least some senators choose to defect, rather than cooperate, in the crafting of public goods. In the Senate such difficulties are largely captured by the buzzword *unpredictability*, with senators and staff often calling for a more "family-friendly schedule" or fewer night-time roll calls. As Senator Robert Bennett (R-Utah) reported in 1997 after surveying half his colleagues as chair of a Senate reform task force, every senator save one complained about the unpredictability of the Senate.[31] Unpredictability affects staff as well, one of whom noted in a survey that his life "is at the total mercy of the hours of the Senate and the unpredictability of the Senate."[32] The unpredictability of the Senate, combined with senators' heavy workloads and conflicting time pressures, led Senator Robert Byrd (D-W.V.) to testify in 1993 that the "root problem plaguing the Senate today [is] what I would term the 'fractured attention' of Senators.'"[33] The chamber's collective action problems are not, in other words, simply a function of senators' conflicting ambitions and priorities. Chamber rules and practices significantly affect the chamber's ability to coordinate its business on the floor.

How might the severity of such conditions be monitored in a checkup? One approach would be to focus on floor outcomes: What happens to bills that have made it onto the chamber's floor agenda? What percentage is eventually passed by the Senate and what percentage is eventually enacted into law? An alternative is to focus on floor process: How many quorum votes occur? What is the balance between procedural and policy votes? How often are cloture motions filed and voted on? How many cloture votes occur per measure? How often do they succeed?

Such measures would provide some sense of the Senate's decisionmaking capacities, but the caveat about interpretation needs to be raised again. As I explore below, measures of floor productivity are likely to be contentious so long as there is significant disagreement over salient issues. One person's gridlock, after all, is another's preferred legislative outcome. Of course, even a person's own vital signs are not necessarily interpretable out of context. As in medicine, careful attention to context should occur in monitoring floor decisionmaking in the Senate. High levels of unsuccessful cloture votes and repeated cloture motions on a single measure probably should worry us more in a Senate with a large unfinished agenda than in a chamber with little on its legislative plate. Similarly, high levels of bipartisanship on minor issues might tell us little about the strength of working relationships across the partisan aisle; high levels of bipartisanship on major issues might instead be more important in reading the results of an institutional checkup.

Bicameral Coordination

Collective action problems are also likely to arise when the two chambers meet to resolve differences in conference. Achieving bicameral coordination can be quite difficult because of the array of contending interests at play. First, members of the conference may or may not reflect the preferences of their chambers at large, and both chambers must eventually approve a conference report.[34] Second, the policy views of the two chambers may be sufficiently different to forestall bicameral agreement. Indeed, intrachamber disagreements can be a potent source of legislative gridlock.[35] Even when the two chambers are controlled by the same party, bicameral coordination can be difficult, as evidenced by the inability of a Republican House and Senate to agree on managed care and bankruptcy reforms, gun control, prescription drug coverage, and tax cut proposals in the 106th Congress (1999–2000). Even under unified government at the start of the 107th Congress, House and Senate negotiators were unable to reach easy agreement in conference on a salient education package. Third, Senate rules that allow extended debate on the three motions required to appoint conferees and go to conference further exacerbate bicameral coordination by increasing the influence of individuals and minority coalitions over the shape of bicameral agreements.

A number of indicators might be used to gauge institutional health at the bicameral stage. These might include the frequency and success of cloture votes on motions related to conferences and conference reports, the amount of time elapsed between House and Senate passage of competing bills and the convening or completion of conference, and the percentage of salient measures stalemating at the bicameral stage. Each of these measures might give some indication of congressional and Senate capacity for resolving differences at the bicameral stage.

The "Member Enterprise"

Robert Salisbury and Kenneth Shepsle coined the term the "member enterprise" in evaluating the organization of members' personal offices.[36] The state of the member enterprise arguably affects the ability of senators and their staffs to manage their workloads and time demands and thus helps to shape senators' ability to participate effectively in chamber decisionmaking. The more difficult it is for senators and their staffs to meet obligations and conflicting demands, the more likely collective action problems will emerge in the chamber.

Some such demands were explored earlier in discussing committee workloads and the unpredictability of the Senate. More generally, we should be concerned about senators' *time budgets*: the number of demands and the time available to meet them. Here Rudman's concerns about the amount of time spent fund-raising come to the fore because fund-raising imposes a significant constraint on senators' ability to participate fully in legislative life. True, the number and size of senators' campaign contributions, as well as the amount of money needed to wage a successful campaign, vary significantly by state size and other factors.[37] However, the more time a senator spends fund-raising the less easy it is for him or her to schedule work in the Senate, and the less time senators have to spend in the chamber together, both of which arguably hamper coordination in the Senate. Time constraints also limit senators' ability to study issues before them, let alone read bills before votes on their passage, again affecting the ability of senators to be effective participants in crafting public law.

A final aspect of the institutional checkup should delve into the time budgets of senators and their staffs, with an eye to determining how senators allocate their time among competing demands. Such a measure might be obtained through routine surveys of senators and their staffs, although senators may be unwilling to admit how much time they spend fund-raising and underreport it. Finally, some way of measuring senators' and staff workloads would be desirable, as a means of gauging the size and scope of demands facing the Senate. Such workload tallies might include the number of issues on the public agenda, constitutional demands such as pending treaties and nominations submitted by the president, and constituency-based demands such as requests for assistance and state appearances. Comparing House and Senate indicators on such measures (save the constitutional ones) would be informative because it might provide a means of evaluating how well legislative workloads and responsibilities are divided between the chambers.

A Sample Indicator

The potential checkup indicators offered here fall into one of two categories: process or output. The process variables all tap aspects of the internal operation of the Senate, essentially gauging the level of activity in the Senate and the activities of its members. Thus when we monitor aspects of floor activity such as the number of quorum calls, cloture votes, and so forth, we are surveying the level and scope of the internal workings of the body. The output measures, in contrast, attempt to capture the performance of the Senate and its component parts. Thus when we monitor the Senate through the percentage of bills that die in committee or on the floor or in conference, we are essentially evaluating the contours of Senate decisionmaking and the chamber's ultimate performance.

Interestingly, when scholars and practitioners were brought together at an early stage of this project, they were far more enthusiastic about measures that track outcomes than about those that track process.[38] As former House member Tony Beilenson argued, indicators likely to capture the public's attention are unlikely to include measures of the inner workings of the chamber. Instead, Beilenson recommended judging the Congress on the basis of some measure of "how well the Congress is dealing with, either reacting to or leading on, some of the major problems facing the country," envisioning a score card "listing important issues of the day and whether . . . Congress is addressing them." Beilenson's comments were echoed by others such as veteran Senate staff member Bill Dauster, who recommended determining the major issues in the public's eye and then determining Congress's record in addressing them. Such an indicator would provide a sense, in the words of political scientist Michael Malbin, of "whether Congress is doing its job, which is a job after all of collective deliberation . . . for the country."[39]

I propose as sample indicators two measures of Senate and congressional output. The first monitors the Senate's performance in addressing salient issues on the public agenda; the second measures each Congress's record in enacting laws that affect those issues by the time it adjourns. The latter measure has already been developed and tested and comports nicely with the received record of legislative performance in the second half of the twentieth century.[40] The performance measure extracts a list of nationally important issues from the editorial pages of the *New York Times* each Congress and determines whether Congress enacted significant legislation to address the issue. The proposed Senate measure would monitor the Senate's performance on these same issues, noting the percentage of issues that fail to be addressed by the Senate. Together the measures provide a means of monitoring Senate and congressional performance on the important issues of the day, indicators of the Senate's decisionmaking capacity, and its ability to overcome collective action problems endemic to the chamber.

The measure was most recently refined for the 106th Congress (1999–2000). That Congress faced fourteen salient issues (as defined by the issues addressed on the editorial page of the *New York Times*) and deadlocked on over half of them (including campaign finance reform, gun control, and managed health care reform). Congress deadlocked on ten of the salient issues, yielding a performance score (or more aptly a gridlock score) of 70 percent. To put these scores into perspective, Congress deadlocked on only 26 percent (six of twenty-three issues) in the 80th Congress (1947–48). The 104th Congress had a gridlock score of

42 percent, deadlocking on eight of nineteen salient issues. The rise in gridlock between the 104th and 106th Congresses comports with our sense of differences between the two Congresses: the 104th ended with a raft of legislative accomplishments in the run-up to the 1996 elections, as Congress enacted major legislation on welfare reform, telecommunications, lobbying reform, water quality, and several other issues. In contrast, the 106th was noted for its much slimmer record, with its highlights limited to debt relief abroad, protecting the Everglades, and granting trading status to China.

There are hazards, to be sure, in monitoring a legislative chamber by its output because a sign of healthy, collaborative decisionmaking might be an agreement not to pass legislation. Still, the issues that make it onto the *Times*'s radar screen and merit frequent discussion on its editorial pages tend to be issues of high public salience and issues that reappear on others' agendas, such as those of congressional party leaders. Thus, evaluating a chamber on its ability to reach decisions on salient public problems is a reasonable and appropriate—though surely not uncontroversial—way to monitor the health of a legislative institution.

Concluding Thoughts

It is not easy to monitor the health of national institutions. Such efforts presuppose some consensus about what constitutes a healthy body and require indicators that may be impossible to build. Acknowledging the limits of the endeavor, such evaluations are still important to attempt if we value the health of representative government and the public's ability to make such judgments.

Given the pitfalls of the endeavor, and in particular the difficulty of devising and interpreting indicators of institutional health, I have focused here on the concrete problem of collective action in the Senate. Surveying critical junctures of decisionmaking, I have probed the areas in which the Senate typically encounters problems coordinating the productive participation of its members and suggested ways of evaluating how well the Senate achieves its role of collective decisionmaking. To the extent that the Senate avoids common pitfalls of collective action, it will be reflected in the sample gridlock indicators offered above. And the better the Senate's performance, the greater confidence we should have in the Senate's capacity for deliberative governance.

In this endeavor I am assuming that a consensus exists on the importance of securing collective action: representative bodies should be able to reach decisions in a timely fashion, with the widespread participation of their members. There are occasions, of course, when deliberation should be slow and inaction a preferable outcome. Still, it is not far-fetched to argue that legislatures work best when they eventually reach decisions with the broad assent of their members, no matter what those decisions might be. If so, the Senate's ability to set an agenda, complete its deliberations, and respond to major public problems of the day seem like reasonable grounds on which to evaluate its health and well-being. If a chamber is unable to channel the ambitions and energies of its members to address major public dilemmas, it is likely failing to achieve the collective action necessary for creating and maintaining public goods.

This brings us full circle back to Warren Rudman's observations about life in the contemporary Senate. To place his concerns in theoretical perspective, partisanship and individualism are harmful to the chamber and the ambitions of its members because they suggest *endemic problems of collective action*: a lot of motion, but not much action. Our empirical challenge is to find a way of distinguishing between motion and action, between legislative activities that demonstrate a healthy legislative process and those that suggest a chamber just spinning its wheels. Quantitative indicators may fail to provide the nuance we are looking for, raising the need for some qualitative measurement of the Senate's success and failure in fostering and completing deliberation. However monitored, an institutional checkup that assesses the state of collective action in the Senate is a necessary step in evaluating the strength and capacity of national institutions.

Notes

1. Interview with Warren Rudman, Washington, D.C., June 12, 1997.

2. See Warren Rudman, *Combat: Twelve Years in the Senate* (Random House, 1996), pp. 254–45.

3. Alan Rosenthal, "The Good Legislature: Getting beyond 'I Know It When I See It.'" Legislative Studies Section Newsletter (www.apsanet.org/%7Elss/Newsletter/jul98/rosenthal.html [accessed August 21, 2002]).

4. Keith Krehbiel, "The Good Legislature from a Positivist Perspective." Legislative Studies Section Newsletter (www.apsanet.org/%7Elss/Newsletter/jul98/krehbiel.html [accessed August 21, 2002]).

5. Rosenthal, "The Good Legislature."

6. Morris P. Fiorina, *Congress: Keystone of the Washington Establishment*, 2d ed. (Yale University Press, 1989).

7. Steven S. Smith, *Call to Order* (Brookings, 1989).

8. Rosenthal, "The Good Legislature."

9. Malcolm Jewell, "Political Dimensions of a 'Good Legislature,'" Legislative Studies Section Newsletter (www.apsanet.org/%7Elss/Newsletter/jul98/jewell.html [accessed August 21, 2002]).

10. Rosenthal, "The Good Legislature."

11. On voters' views of their members and the institution, see Richard F. Fenno Jr., "If as Ralph Nader Says, Congress Is 'the Broken Branch,' How Come We Love Our Congressmen So Much?" in Norman Ornstein, ed., *Congress in Change: Evolution and Reform* (Praeger, 1975).

12. David Mayhew, *Congress: The Electoral Connection* (Yale University Press, 1974).

13. On legislators' multiple goals, see Richard F. Fenno Jr., *Congressmen in Committees* (Little, Brown, 1973).

14. Jewell, "Political Dimensions of a 'Good Legislature.'"

15. Krehbiel, "The Good Legislature from a Positivist Perspective."

16. William T. Gormley Jr. and David L. Weimer, *Organizational Report Cards* (Harvard University Press, 1999), pp. 61–75.

17. On the relevance of public goods to public action, see, among others, John Aldrich, *Why Parties?* (University of Chicago Press, 1995). Public goods are marked by two characteristics: "nonexcludability" and "jointness of supply." Nonexcludability means that no citizen can be denied the enjoyment of a public good. Clean air, for example, shows nonexcludability since no one (not even polluters) can be enjoined from consuming clean air once it is provided. Jointness of supply simply means that public goods cannot be diminished by one citizen's use or consumption. The concept is classically illustrated by a government-erected lighthouse: one ship's use of the light to avoid the shoreline does not prevent other ships from using the light.

18. See, among others, Mancur Olson, *The Logic of Collective Action* (Harvard University Press, 1966).

19. This assumes that public radio is widely valued as a public good. The illustration does not hinge on the specific example; we might easily substitute a public good with a broader or different constituency.

20. Jewell, "Political Dimensions of a 'Good Legislature.'"

21. See Robert H. Salisbury and Kenneth A. Shepsle, "U.S. Congressman as Enterprise," *Legislative Studies Quarterly*, vol. 6 (November 1981), pp. 559–76.

22. Christopher J. Deering and Steven S. Smith, *Committees in Congress*, 3d ed. (Congressional Quarterly Press, 1997).

23. Joint Committee on the Organization of Congress (JCOC), *Organization of the Congress (Final Report)* (Government Printing Office, 1993), pp. 23–27.

24. As quoted in *Working in Congress* (Congressional Management Foundation, 1995), p. 29.

25. JCOC, *Organization of the Congress*, p. 25.

26. Ibid., p. 263.

27. See Andrew Taylor, "Senate's Partisan Stalemate Has Major Bills Languishing," *Congressional Quarterly Weekly Report*, May 27, 2000.

28. See Andrew Taylor, "Gun Control Vote Provokes Clash between Lott, Daschle over Management of the Senate," *Congressional Quarterly Weekly Report*, May 20, 2000.

29. Despite recent agreements on the treatment of holds, data on holds are unlikely to be released by party leaders. These recent agreements seek to eliminate the secrecy of holds by requiring senators with holds to notify the sponsor of the bill, the committee with jurisdiction, and the majority or minority leader. Senators, however, have already exploited loopholes in the new policy, because neither the sponsor nor committees are required to publicly identify the senator. Further, nominations have no official sponsors and thus appear to fall outside the reach of the policy (although home-state holds on judicial nominees are supposed to be made public). Finally, the majority leader is not required to identify the sponsor. These multiple loopholes allowed Majority Leader Trent Lott to place an anonymous hold on Richard Holbrooke's nomination to be ambassador to the United Nations. See Helen Dewar, "The Senate Has a 'Hold' on Holbrooke," *Washington Post*, July 3, 1999, p. A5.

30. *Working in Congress*, p. 17.

31. The one senator was Bill Frist (R-Tenn.). As a former heart transplant surgeon, Frist noted that the schedule "sounds great to me" (interview with Bennett, May 8, 1997).

32. *Working in Congress*, p. 17.

33. JCOC, *Organization of the Congress*, p. 52.

34. See Kenneth A. Shepsle and Barry Weingast, "Institutional Foundations of Committee Power," *American Political Science Review*, vol. 81 (March 1987), pp. 85–104.

35. Sarah A. Binder, *Stalemate: Causes and Consequences of Legislative Gridlock* (Brookings, 2003).

36. Salisbury and Shepsle, "U.S. Congressman as Enterprise."

37. On the impact of state size, see Frances Lee and Bruce Oppenheimer, *Sizing Up the Senate* (Chicago, 1999).

38. See "Assessing Congress: Drafting an Institutional Report Card," workshop transcript, Woodrow Wilson International Center for Scholars, July 24, 2000.

39. "Assessing Congress," pp. 21–22, 41.

40. See Binder, *Stalemate*.

FOUR

The President's Advisory System: Its Capacity for Governance

KATHRYN DUNN TENPAS

KAREN M. HULT

Although the primary function of the presidency is to execute the law, over time the duties of the office have expanded in significant ways. In the eyes of some observers, the president has gone from wearing many hats to donning too many hats. In order to fulfill their multiple responsibilities, presidents must rely on a highly professional staff organization. Even though the president's staff grew substantially during the second half of the twentieth century, it is not clear whether this expansion always facilitated executive governance. It would be difficult to deny that the aides closest to the president are a major resource for an overcommitted chief executive. Yet the effectiveness and responsiveness of presidential staffs have been questioned on occasion, as has the impact of staff on presidential governance. In order to address such concerns, it may be worthwhile for scholars and observers alike to perform regular "checkups" on the staff.[1] Identifying, collecting data on, and analyzing a comprehensive set of meaningful indicators may reveal the relative "health" of the presidential staff, thereby shedding light on the governing capacity of the presidency.

In what follows, we focus on the president's personal "advisory system." Following Bradley Patterson, we consider this to include aides in the White House Office (WHO) as well as those in the Office of the Vice President, the National Security Council (NSC) staff, the National Economic Council (NEC) staff, and the domestic policy staff.[2] Collectively, these units represent the *primary* policy and political decisionmaking offices most accessible to the president.[3]

65

The discussion proceeds in four stages. We first document the expansion and increasingly pivotal role of presidential staff, making the case for using the "president's advisory system" as the focus of analysis for evaluating the presidency's capacity for governance. Second, we explain the process of evaluating the president's advisory system. Third, we identify key indicators of advisory system health, focusing on a single indicator to demonstrate its ability to tap one aspect of the presidency's governing capacity. Finally, we discuss the implications of our analysis and advocate greater and more routine disclosure in light of the dearth of available data on the president's advisory system.

Why Focus on the President's Advisory System?

Ever since the Brownlow Committee's 1937 statement that the president "needs help," scholars and observers alike have assumed that presidents would benefit from additional staff. Franklin D. Roosevelt's creation of the Executive Office of the President (EOP) in 1939, which included the White House Office, enabled his successors to develop a White House–centered staff apparatus.[4] Although FDR did not expect his successors to continue this expansion, over the next four decades most presidents chose to do so.[5] "In modernizing the presidential office . . . Roosevelt conspicuously avoided planting the seed of the presidential branch; the acquisition of additional White House staff was but a small part in his otherwise ambitious plan to reorganize the presidency."[6] Nevertheless, presidents from Roosevelt through Richard Nixon steadily added more specialized offices, typically increasing the total number of staff members. Interestingly, President Harry Truman is credited with the greatest expansion of the White House staff—a nearly fourfold increase: "This increase was meant to provide a base for policy interests that Truman wished to pursue in the form of an annual presidential legislative program."[7] Since Nixon, presidents have maintained the relative size of the White House staff; although there have been sporadic staff contractions, some administrations have introduced additional specialized offices.[8]

Until the late 1970s, growth of the presidential staff was a sometimes discontinuous process, which began with the addition of vaguely titled assistants to the president and special assistants, many of whom had military backgrounds.[9] After President Johnson, a flurry of new titles appeared such as counselor to the president and assistant to the president for urban affairs. With President Nixon as well came the expansion of the "public

Table 4-1.   *"Title Creep" in the White House*

Administration	Average number of staff titles
Franklin D. Roosevelt[a]	5
Harry S. Truman	13
Dwight D. Eisenhower	29
John F. Kennedy	18
Lyndon B. Johnson	17
Richard M. Nixon	25
Gerald R. Ford[b]	56
James E. Carter	68
Ronald W. Reagan	54
George H. W. Bush	59
William J. Clinton[c]	85

Source: Successive volumes of the *U.S. Government Manual*, 1939–1999/2000.

a. Beginning in 1939.

b. Mostly in response to Watergate and the evident abuse of power by some Nixon staffers, President Ford insisted that the titles of White House aides include specific mention of their assigned responsibilities.

c. Unlike the other volumes for the Clinton administration, the 1993–94 listing does not include "special assistants" to the president. As such, the number of aides listed for that year is substantially lower (forty-five compared to an average of ninety-one for all other years).

relations" presidency, as he and his successors added numerous outreach offices (such as communications, political affairs, public liaison). Meanwhile, other EOP units introduced their own press, legislative liaison, communication, and speechwriting offices.[10]

One manifestation of these additions is the proliferation of titles in the White House Office. Table 4-1 clearly shows the "title creep" that has appeared, largely the result of increasing staff specialization. The sources of growth, while multifaceted, stem primarily from the ease with which presidents can expand their staffs (usually with negligible congressional opposition) and a perception that increasing demands on the institution require a larger staff. In response to a growing array of problems (such as terrorist threats, environmental hazards, increasing crime, a globalizing economy, and new technology), presidents have acquired the means to address myriad issues, and staff members play increasingly influential roles in national security, economic, and domestic policymaking. As a former White House staffer observed: "It is the men and women on the president's personal staff who first channel that power, shape it, focus it—and, on the president's instructions, help him wield it."[11] Put differently, "It is difficult, if not impossible, to imagine how post–New Deal presidents could have responded to the pressures and demands on them without such staff assistance."[12] Furthermore, autobiographical accounts by those who have served in the White House attest to the enormous power wielded by presidential staff members.[13]

As presidents delegate their authority, however, such increased staff influence has come with a price. While modern aides have accrued responsibility, so too have they become increasingly accountable (both legally and publicly) for carrying out presidential directives. Two presidential scandals, Watergate and Iran-contra, boldly illustrate the critical roles played by presidential staff on domestic, political, and foreign policy matters. In both cases, presidential aides indeed were held accountable for their actions. Given the rising threat of congressional and other investigations, it is not at all surprising that numerous senior staff members in the Clinton administration retained personal lawyers. The threat of investigations, of course, also influenced the size of the WHO staff. During the Clinton years, for example, the Office of White House Counsel at times included more than forty lawyers as aides scrambled to respond to attacks on the president. The Reagan White House saw an analogous increase as officials sought to cope with the Iran-contra revelations.[14]

Even so, the Brownlow Committee's prescription for presidential help remains relevant over sixty years later. Assistance is critical to presidents fulfilling their constitutional duties in a context of multiplying responsibilities and ever more vigilant and demanding members of Congress, journalists, and U.S. citizens. Given the pivotal role of the president's advisory system, then, careful scrutiny of its health moves us closer to understanding the governing capacity of the U.S. presidency.

Evaluating the President's Advisory System

In evaluating the health of presidential advisory systems, we emphasize two general criteria: effectiveness and responsiveness. The *effectiveness* of an individual aide (for example, the economic policy adviser), a staff subunit (for example, the counsel's office), or a unit formally placed elsewhere in the Executive Office (such as the National Security Council staff) refers to the degree to which that actor or entity helps advance presidential objectives (by, for instance, providing information or analyses that inform presidential policy decisions or overseeing executive branch implementation of presidential directives). *Responsiveness* refers to staff members' ability and willingness to address the concerns and requests they receive from the president and members of the Washington community (such as members of Congress, executive branch officials, and the media).[15] Members of the Washington community frequently rely upon presidential staff to provide integral assistance and advice in order to fulfill their own responsibilities.[16]

In what follows, we start by applying these two standards to two components of presidential advisory systems: staff composition and staff structures and processes. Staff composition includes the size of the advisory system and its parts as well as individual staff members' qualifications, tenure, working conditions, and job satisfaction. The staff structures and processes component seeks to tap both the capacity of the staff units to fulfill the myriad responsibilities of the president and whether they are structured in ways that enhance decisionmaking. Relatedly, attention focuses on whether formal procedures are in place that enable presidents to receive adequate information and advisory input from relevant sources while avoiding both presidential overload and isolation.

A First Cut: Applying the Criteria

Various dimensions of *staff composition* may boost effectiveness. First, adequately sized staff units appear to be important.[17] Despite frequent complaints about "bloated" White House staffs, considerable evidence indicates that such concerns may be overstated, or at least accurate for only some units some of the time.[18] Suggested in turn is the need to *disaggregate* data on staff size by, for example, subunit and nature of employees (distinguishing between, for example, career and noncareer, professional and nonprofessional aides) in order to appreciate more fully the impact of changes in staff size on effectiveness.

Also likely to be relevant to effectiveness are the experience and expertise of individual staffers and the mix of staff backgrounds. The wisdom of not building a presidential staff operation solely around campaign aides now seems well accepted.[19] Similarly, particular jobs (such as, congressional liaison or associate counsel) have certain requisite professional backgrounds.

The extent of turnover (or, more positively, the length of tenure) of presidential staffers may influence effectiveness as well.[20] To the degree that "institutional memory" is important, effectiveness, and ultimately presidential decisionmaking capacity, will be weakened if aides stay in specific positions, in particular subunits, or in an administration for only short periods of time.[21]

In addition, working conditions appear likely to be linked to effectiveness, both directly by enhancing staff ability and willingness to perform particular tasks and indirectly by affecting job satisfaction. Inadequate computer hardware, software, and technical support, for instance, may compromise an aide's or a unit's ability to discover, assemble, analyze, or communicate policy and political information. Over extended periods, long hours, high pressure, and limited time off may hurt individuals' judgment and efficiency, problems often exacerbated by accompanying damage to staffers' personal lives.

Poor or deteriorating working conditions may also, of course, reduce job satisfaction.[22] Low or declining job satisfaction, in turn, may undermine effectiveness (by, for example, reducing commitment to one's job or weakening relations with other staffers). Material incentives (such as salary and benefits) may be less important for presidential staff, perhaps especially early in administrations and at very junior and very senior levels. Nonetheless, pay inequities, minimal salary increases, or relatively low salaries may have corrosive effects on staffers.[23] So too may perceptions of unfair distribution of "perks" (time off, access to the White House mess, invitations to state dinners, and the like). Staffers' sense of involvement in the overall work of an administration also should not be overlooked. Katherine Higgins, President Clinton's cabinet secretary, observed: "If there is no regular way to manage the affairs of the White House so that everyone feels part of it and knows what is happening, people will go off on their own and try to figure it out the best they can. That's very dangerous and counterproductive."[24]

Although staff composition and size appear to be important primarily for effectiveness, they also can affect responsiveness.[25] Criticism of staff size by congressional committees and the associated demands for cuts may well hamper effectiveness and ultimately undermine presidential capacity.[26] At the same time, the larger and the more specialized staffs become, the more difficult it is for presidents (and chiefs of staff) to determine whether and how their directives are being followed or presidential goals pursued. Moreover, it is often very difficult for congressional committees, journalists, and others to get information on exactly who works in which White House Office and Executive Office positions, for what salary, and with which status (for example, detailee or regular, longer-term, or political appointee). Yet necessary for at least a minimum level of responsiveness to Congress and to the public is a more *transparent* advisory system, where information may be obtained about, for example, the balance between detailees and more permanent staff as well as the size of units and subunits in the EOP.[27]

The second component of presidential advisory systems—staff structures and procedures—also is relevant to concerns about effectiveness and responsiveness. Seemingly most important for judging effectiveness are the "representativeness" and the "procedural rationality" of the advisory system's decision arrangements. Decision structures and procedures are more representative the more they include officials who reflect the range of relevant policy or political expertise and experience.[28] Procedural rationality increases when "decision makers explore divergent information and perspectives within the constraints of available time and cognitive capacities *and* are able to reach decision closure."[29] Although staff decision processes with these characteristics clearly cannot guarantee "better" outcomes, they arguably do increase the likelihood that presidents will have access to credible information and analysis, and to useful advice.[30]

Moreover, desirable staff structures and procedures should perform well on the second evaluative standard, responsiveness. For aides to be responsive to the president (and to senior staffers acting on the president's behalf), there should be clear chains of command within and across EOP units that staffers both know about and follow. To bolster responsiveness to members of Congress and the public, more general knowledge about how decisions are made and which parties are involved—another form of transparency—evidently is needed.

Yet this standard may be both somewhat less important than effectiveness and frequently difficult to apply. Although staff structuring and processes should be responsive to input from the president, they should not be excessively responsive to the demands and concerns of members of the Washington community. Staff members must walk a fine line between showing conscientious concern for these publics and not allowing external demands to jeopardize their effectiveness and overall job performance. For example, while interest groups clamor for briefings with White House staff members, it is impossible for White House officials to meet with every constituency group. More critically, we would argue that interest group access to White House staff should not come at the cost of favoring specific groups, as, for example, formulation of Bill Clinton's health care plan and George W. Bush's energy proposals allegedly did. Here, too, one must be careful about painting with too broad a brush. For instance, some contend that, even as the presidency has grown *too* permeable to specialized interests, it has become less open and attentive to members of Congress and, especially, careerists in the executive branch.[31] Determining the degree to which White House staff members should respond to particular members of the Washington community can be a vexing task because the variation in sensitivity, timing, and other factors prevents easy generalization. This criterion, while significant, often will be problematic in specific applications.

Different Perspectives

Not surprisingly, judgments about the effectiveness and responsiveness of a presidential advisory system may well differ, depending on the judge.[32] An evaluation of presidential advisory systems, for example, might judge staff performance from the viewpoint of the staff members, the president, and the Washington community. Presumably, for staff members to be effective, they must enjoy desirable conditions, which include receiving adequate compensation, working in a supportive physical environment, and having a sense of job satisfaction. Similarly, presidents need to recruit aides skilled in the arts of coalition building, policymaking, public persuasion, and the ways of Washington. Meanwhile, the Washington community's views of staff effectiveness and responsiveness can be crucial for presidential success with legislative initiatives, policy implementation, and the mobilization and maintenance of public support.

The next section identifies indicators of staff performance from each vantage point, examining both components of the presidential advisory system in the context of the three evaluative standards. In doing this we move closer to answering questions such as the following. Do presidential staff members possess the requisite experience, education, and political savvy to facilitate presidential governance? Do these aides stay in their positions throughout the president's tenure, or is there frequent turnover with the consequent loss of institutional memory? Are staffs organized in such a way that they can generate high-quality information and advice under pressing time constraints? For those outside 1600 Pennsylvania Avenue, do members of Congress, civil servants, political appointees, and the Washington media find staff members proficient in their executive duties? Can members of the Washington community easily learn who works in the White House and how decisions are made? Answers to such questions can help in assessing the health of the personal presidential advisory system.

Utopia versus Reality: The Not-So-Perfect Advisory System

We begin by envisioning the "perfect" advisory system—that is, by identifying some of the features that appear to be especially important to presi-

Table 4-2. *Evaluative Components and Qualities of an "Ideal" Presidential Advisory System*

Perspective	Staff composition	Staff structures and processes
Effectiveness		
Staff members	Sufficient staff members; mix of campaign and government experience; relevant professional background and training; low turnover; good working conditions; access to president or senior staff; high job satisfaction	Policy specialization; inclusion where staff have relevant expertise or experience
President	Requisite knowledge and skills; low turnover	High procedural rationality; representative processes
Washington community	Well informed; sensitive to institutional constraints; honest broker	Logical, comprehensible processes; access to policy experts; clear chain of command
Responsiveness		
Staff members	Access to president or senior staff	Awareness of and adherence to procedures
President	Knowledge of and access to appropriate staff; loyalty; low turnover	Adherence to formal procedures
Washington community	Provision of requested information; honest broker	Logical, comprehensible processes; clear chain of command; access to policy experts; representative processes

dential governance (see table 4-2). Then we examine the realities of presidential staffing. What we find is that the existing staff system falls short of our ideals. Determining whether this is true only under certain presidents, at particular points in a presidential term, or in all contemporary presidencies requires additional information and analysis. The discussion suggests indicators that, if collected and analyzed on a regular basis, would provide more insight into continuities and changes in staff performance.

Staff Composition

Every president dreams of having a highly skilled White House staff capable of fulfilling multiple tasks simultaneously in an environment that encourages collegiality and loyalty. In this ideal world, staff members would be well compensated for their prestigious jobs. They would have ample support staff in state-of-the-art offices, work regular hours, and be able to take vacations. In addition, the most senior members would have sufficient access to the president for candid discussions of policy options and politics. The last major component of this ideal staff concerns their relationships with the Washington community. Presidential aides would be well informed, sensitive to institutional constraints, and able and willing to explore opposing policy alternatives and strategies; and when policy conflicts arose, they would serve as honest brokers.

In reality, few of these ideal characteristics are present. Anecdotal evidence suggests that White House aides deal with myriad problems, among them damaging staff leaks to the press, high rates of turnover, limited workspace, little personal time, a brutally competitive work environment, lack of access to the president, the mounting threat of having to pay for legal advice, and relatively poor compensation.[33] As for presidential perceptions of the staff, chief executives are burdened by the occasional unqualified staffer, tenuous loyalty, high turnover rates, and increasing difficulty attracting first-rate employees (because of, for example, burdensome ethics requirements, intrusive background checks, and meager compensation). Finally, members of the Washington community sometimes find the president's staff to be contentious, uncooperative, and pompous, as well as disrespectful of careerists, some members of Congress, and political appointees.

Given the disparity between the ideal and reality, to what extent are the negative features endemic to the presidency or more idiosyncratic? In an effort to make such distinctions, we propose numerous indicators.

From the staff perspective:

—Job satisfaction. Examine interview excerpts (and the associated analyses) from the White House 2001 Project,[34] Miller Center interviews, and exit interviews conducted (through 1992) by officials from the National Archives and housed at presidential libraries. Note the various and frequent discussions of quality-of-life issues, job frustrations, and the like. See also relevant staff memoirs and *National Journal* ("White House Notebook," "People") and *Washington Post* ("In the Loop") accounts of staff departures and promotions.

—Compensation. Obtain staff salary data. Congress has passed legislation requiring the publication of staff salary data "for official use only."[35] Obtaining these figures (currently available in some form in annual presidential budgets and in appropriations subcommittee hearings) would provide insight into the disparities between public and private sector salaries. As noted earlier, however, in many cases, particularly at the beginning of

Life
compensation)

an administration, compensation does not affect recruitment nearly as much as it does later in the term.

—Personal data and time-consuming forms. Track the increasing demands on senior White House staff members to provide revealing personal financial information or spend time filling out background security forms. For some prospective White House staff members, this may play more of a decisive role than compensation in determining whether to serve a president.[36]

—Job tenure. Track the tenure in selected staff positions, subunits, and administrations. Possible sources include the *U.S. Government Manual*, official phone books, White House press releases, staff directories,[37] and the *National Journal* and *Washington Post* features mentioned earlier.

From the president's perspective: Of interest here are both whether presidents are satisfied with their aides' loyalty, responsiveness, experience, and capabilities and whether available data indicate that staffers are likely to serve presidents well or poorly. The following are examples of the information sources that may be especially useful.

—Accounts of participants and observers. Presidential and staff memoirs contain retrospective accounts, while more contemporaneous views can be noted in staff reorganization documents, other internal memos, leaked criticisms, and other documents.

—Information on staff recruitment. To what extent do presidents hire the "best and the brightest"?[38] Biographical data can be obtained on senior staff to determine the level and nature of their experience (for example, age, educational background, past government service, and relevant business and nonprofit experience). Possible sources include *Who's Who*, *National Journal* "Decisionmaker" editions,[39] *Washington Monthly*, staff directories, electronic White House press releases pertaining to new hires, and materials at presidential libraries (for example, in White House staff files). This information can reveal a president's ability to recruit not just those with appropriate policy or political expertise, but also those most experienced in dealing with the Washington community. Of related concern may be the extent of reliance on detailees and interns instead of regular aides to perform particular kinds of tasks.[40]

—Evidence on staff turnover. Dickinson and Tenpas report staff turnover rates from 1929 through 1997.[41] Data also might be compiled from successive volumes of the *U.S. Government Manual* and White House phone books to determine turnover rates. The *National Journal* and *Wash-*

ington Post might provide supplemental information (such as reasons for staff departures). Increasing turnover and differential turnover among units might point to efficiency problems as well as to deterioration in staff effectiveness and institutional memory.[42]

From the Washington community's perspective: Here, the focus shifts to community members' perceptions of staff effectiveness and responsiveness. It should be underscored that the results would need to be interpreted carefully, since a significant increase in negative views might be at least partly attributable to heightened media scrutiny, more polarized partisan debate, and added statutory and administration ethics requirements.

—Press reports. A Nexis search could determine the number of positive, negative, and neutral stories about presidents' senior staff (such as those about scandals, cabinet members' comments about staff incompetence or staff blocking access to the president, congressional complaints about staff overreaching). Periodicals such as the *National Journal, Congressional Quarterly Weekly Report, Roll Call,* and *Washington Monthly* also might be expected to produce helpful information. All would provide examples of how the staff may or may not be serving the Washington community or the president. Longitudinal comparisons both within and across administrations might reveal increasing frequencies of reported staff missteps (perhaps as aides grow more embattled in a term or journalists become increasingly critical over several terms).[43]

—Interviews. Interviews with White House journalists, association executives, and lobbyists, focusing on their first hand experiences with the White House staff, would shed light on performance.

—Appropriations hearings. Such hearings may include comments or expressions of concerns about particular White House units or staffing patterns.

Staff Structures and Processes

Independent of staff members' perceptions of satisfaction, the president's concern with whether aides are loyal or experienced, or the judgments of members of the Washington community, attention also may focus on how well organized the president's staff is. Are appropriate procedures and established norms in place, providing adequate information to the president and promoting efficient, effective, and timely decisionmaking? Is the president's advisory system specialized enough to provide policy expertise and structured in such a way to facilitate collegiality and cooperation among offices? Are there clear chains of command as well as mechanisms for coordinating the activities of specialized units and for resolving disputes? Again, to add clarity, we return to a discussion of the ideal and the reality.

What should White House staff structuring look like? From a staff member's perspective, no single unit should be understaffed. Each office should employ staff with policy and political specialization and expertise and the capacity to perform multiple tasks. Senior staff members from all units should be afforded adequate access to the president or the chief of staff. In addition, staff members should be aware and informed of formal procedures and follow them as directed.[44]

The staff sometimes appears to be overly specialized, inadequately coordinated, and too permeable to external interests. Some units are marginalized by certain leaders and according to the president's proclivities. From the staff members' perspective, frustrations may reflect the absence of a single chain of command if decisions involve several offices; such multilayered decisionmaking complicates the process, reduces its efficiency, and makes coordination difficult. Some offices lack sufficient employees and expertise. Cronyism and campaign favors result in inappropriate hiring and poorly run offices. Formal procedures are often cumbersome, not clearly defined, or not enforced. At times, presidential preferences and time constraints minimize or even prevent adherence to formal procedures, thereby jeopardizing their legitimacy.

From the president's perspective, responsiveness and effectiveness (procedural rationality and the representation of differing viewpoints) again are important. The advisory system should be composed of a sufficient number of skilled staff members capable of accomplishing multiple tasks in a timely manner. It should be capable of providing maximum information while minimizing infighting, turf battles, and jurisdictional questions. The staff hierarchy should be clearly defined and reliable; the chain of command should be routinely used. Formal procedures should facilitate timely decisionmaking and provide the president with the best information possible from all relevant sources given the constraints of time and other priorities.

Not surprisingly, staff structuring and processes frequently fall short of the ideal for sitting presidents. There often may be too many incentives for staff members to agree with the president. Staff infighting can reduce the president's ability to obtain adequate information before making a decision. Multiple constituency-related offices may make decisionmaking too permeable to outside interest groups. Formal processes are not always conducive to timely decisionmaking or adaptable to unusual or volatile circumstances.

The members of the Washington community rely on specific offices to respond in a timely manner. These outsiders prefer direct communication with policy experts and those close to the president, and they need to be able to recognize the chain of command within offices and across the administration. Finally, formal internal processes for executive decisionmaking should be comprehensible to the outsider.

Yet sometimes units' jurisdictions overlap and a defined staff hierarchy appears to be absent. Changes in decision processes, shifting issue positions, and other demands make the interested outsiders' task a challenge, helping perpetuate the perception that staff members are less honest brokers than advocates. This situation is exacerbated when, from time to time, formal procedures change without notice or are nothing short of incomprehensible to those outside.

The following indicators may be useful in evaluating staff structures and processes.

From the staff perspective:

—Data on the size of subunits within the WHO and in the other selected offices of the EOP.[45]

—Key structural developments (such as specialization, number of staff units, ratio of public relations to policy units and staffers), measured by the number and type of units that have been added to and removed from the White House Office and the other key units within the Executive Office of the President.[46] Useful as well may be scholarly works that address issues pertaining to White House staff specialization, organization, and decision and advisory processes.[47]

From the president's perspective:

—Evidence of efforts to circumvent formal procedures. Both scholarly works and primary sources may be useful. Case studies of particular decisions may aid in determining the procedural rationality and representativeness of formal decisionmaking processes.

—Relevant staff accounts and interviews. Such information might lend insight into the causes of staff infighting and tendencies to agree with the chief executive.

From the Washington community's perspective:

—Documents by political insiders that discuss instances of frustration with formal White House decisionmaking processes (or the lack of explicit procedures).

—Primary sources (such as Web information and press accounts) for descriptions of staff responsibilities and decisionmaking processes. Tracking the frequency of such stories would help to determine the extent to which the White House keeps members of the Washington community aware of this type of information. (Table 4-3 summarizes these indicators of effectiveness.)

Missing Data

In addition we have identified a number of currently unavailable indicators that also might prove useful in conducting an institutional checkup.

—Surveys of current and former White House senior staff about the quality of the work environment and their overall job satisfaction.[48]

—Surveys of the Washington community (of members of Congress, congressional staff, senior civil servants, journalists, and other outsiders with known connections to the presidency) about their perceptions and expectations of presidential staff performance and about how to satisfy their demands and improve communication.

—Regularly collected and publicly reported data on the types of employees *within* the WHO, the vice president's office, and the staffs of the NSC and the Office of Policy Development, including detailees, more permanent staff, and presidential appointees.

—Regularly collected and publicly reported data on the precise dates of staff hires and departures. Unusually high staff turnover might point to dissatisfaction among presidential advisers and the negative side effects of decreased efficiency and loss of institutional memory.

—Publicly available comprehensive data on staff size and staff salaries for comparison with for-profit, nonprofit, and other governmental positions.

—Data revealing staff adherence to formal decisionmaking procedures, the efficiency of such processes, and rates of and reasons for circumvention. Documents, interviews, and analyses examined retrospectively likely would be most appropriate here. Possible examples of such work include Burke and Greenstein's study of decisionmaking related to U.S. troop commitment in Vietnam under Presidents Eisenhower and Johnson; Moens's evaluation of four cases of foreign policy decisionmaking under President Carter; and Ponder's examination of domestic information and advising processes in the Carter White House.[49]

It would be especially valuable in our view to regularly and systematically collect these sorts of data and make them available in a timely and

Table 4-3. *Illustrative Indicators of the Relative Health of Presidential Advisory Systems*

Staff composition	Staff structures and processes

Effectiveness

Staffers' job satisfaction: comments on "quality-of-life" issues, job frustrations (in, for example, White House 2001 interviews, Miller Center interviews, staff memoirs, press accounts of staff departures and promotions)	Size of WHO subunits and selected EOP offices: track number of staff over time within and across administrations (through, for example, OPM, annual reports under White House Personnel Authorization-Employment Act of 1978, scholarly works)
Compensation: salary figures in annual budgets and appropriations subcommittee hearings; compare salaries to senior federal executive salaries (available from OPM) and earnings of for-profit and nonprofit executives (available from Economic Policy Institute, Bureau of Labor Statistics)	Specialization: extent to which individual aides and specific units primarily perform particular tasks (such as speechwriting or advising on trade policy) and the degree to which they are the main people or units performing the task. Measured initially by, for example, counting the number and type of subunits, tasks, and people that have been added to and removed from the WHO, the vice president's office, and White House policy staffs. Press reports and scholarly works on White House staff specialization and decisionmaking also may be useful.
Background and experience: information on age, educational degrees, past governmental and other work experience (from, for example, *Who's Who, National Journal* "Decisionmaker" editions, press releases, presidential libraries)	Coordination: extent to which coordinating mechanisms exist (and are used) to link specialized subunits and individuals; examples include formal staff positions such as chief of staff and staff secretary; more ad hoc meetings, legislative task forces, and regular, informal senior staff sessions (such as the Blair House Group in Reagan's first term, Karl Rove's "strategery" group)
Job tenure: time in specific staff positions, subunits, administrations (using, for example, *U.S. Government Manual*, official phone books, *Capitol Source*, press accounts)	Representativeness: extent to which specific presidential decision processes include those aides with relevant political or policy experience and expertise
President's perceptions of staff effectiveness (conveyed in, for example, presidential and staff memoirs, staff reorganization documents, other internal memos and e-mails)	Procedural rationality: extent to which specific presidential decision processes include those aides with relevant political or policy experience and expertise; whether decision is made in a timely fashion (using, for example, contemporaneous press reports, documents in presidential libraries, interviews with participants)

continues

Staff composition	*Staff structures and processes*
Washington community's perceptions of staff effectiveness (found in, e.g., national and international press reports of comments on levels of staff competence, political skill, policy expertise; similar reports in Washington-based periodicals such as *Congressional Quarterly Weekly Reports, National Journal, Roll Call*)	

Responsiveness

Presidential perceptions of staff responsiveness to presidential objectives, directives: presidential comments about, reports on presidential views of responsiveness of individual aides, staff subunits (found in presidential documents and memoirs, media reports)	Staff awareness of and adherence to formal procedures: reports of White House staffers (expressed, for example, in internal memos, oral histories, memoirs); reports and comments in press by members of Congress, congressional staff, agency and department officials, interest group representatives
Washington community perceptions of staff reactions to their needs or demands (and the variation in such perceptions among members of the community): congressional, agency official, press, interest group comments (found, for example, in news stories, interviews, newsletters, presidential documents)	Clear chain of command: reports and comments in press, in congressional subcommittee and committee reports, by the General Accounting Office(GAO), in interest group communication about how decisions are made and evidence of chains of command; perceptions of White House aides (expressed, for example, in internal memos, oral histories, memoirs); scholarly analyses of specific decisions and decision processes
	Washington community access to information: reports in press, in congressional subcommittee and committee reports, by GAO about readiness of access to requested information

understandable fashion for analysis by journalists, scholars, and citizens. Currently such data appear only sporadically (when they are produced by individual scholars or the White House Interview Program, for example) and when they are likely to be skewed to what is new, dramatic, or scandalous.

Illustration: Turnover among Presidential Advisers

Analyzing a single indicator may help illustrate how information about the presidential staff can contribute to an examination of presidential gov-

Figure 4-1. *Mean White House Staff Retention Rates, 1929–97*

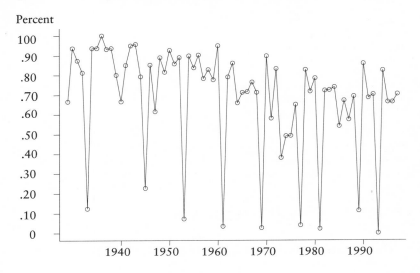

Percent

erning capacity. This section briefly examines turnover among presidential advisers.

Bruce
Reed
Gene
Sporki

During President Clinton's first term, the White House staff and cabinet underwent a substantial makeover. The *U.S. Government Manual* reveals that of the twenty-three aides with titles signifying senior status, fewer than half (eleven) served the entire four years, and only five of the twenty-three stayed in their original posts. Observers usually attributed this turnover to a specific controversy (such as a scandal or an ethical lapse), burnout, or the administration's inability to hire experienced staff members. However, absent further support, such explanations are merely anecdotal and speculative.

In an effort to provide a more systematic explanation of staff turnover, Dickinson and Tenpas examined turnover rates among the president's advisers from 1929 through 1997.[50] They focused on two elements of the president's advisory system: the White House Office and the secretaries of the major executive branch departments that constitute the presidential cabinet. Cabinet secretaries were included because they were the primary source of advice to presidents in the early years and remained influential in varying degrees as the White House staff expanded. Relying on the *U.S. Government Manual*, the most comprehensive single source of long-term (1929 to the present) senior White House Office and cabinet listings at the individual level, Dickinson and Tenpas calculated the mean staff retention rates from 1929 through 1997.[51] These rates compared the numbers of presidential aides and cabinet members that remained from one year to the next. As figure 4-1 shows, there has been a relatively steady decline punctuated by periods of complete staff turnover due to the advent of a new administration.

Staff turnover can cause myriad problems for presidents. Effectiveness may be compromised by the loss of institutional memory when experienced aides leave. The losses escalate if senior aides take other staff members with them when they depart. Meanwhile, efficiency may drop as other aides are required to recruit, hire, and train replacements. In addition, the disruption of previous lines of internal and external staff communication may for a time reduce both effectiveness and responsiveness. Of course, some turnover is to be expected, and it may even be desirable as a means of injecting new ideas and energy into an administration or of easing out less competent or less responsive aides. In any event, these data indicate a steady decline in the tenure of White House staff and cabinet members, a phenomenon that likely deserves serious attention.

Conclusion

The U.S. presidency is noteworthy for many reasons, not the least of which is its breadth of authority and responsibility, particularly since FDR and continuing into the twenty-first century. Its expansive role in the American polity has heightened the influence and range of involvement of presidential staff members. The centrality of the president's advisory system is an enduring feature of the modern presidency that deserves further study and evaluation. Given the growing responsibility of presidential advisers, the nature and the extent of their participation in the presidency should be far more transparent than it has been. The glaring absence of data on presidential staff members and staff structuring and procedures and the difficulty of obtaining basic information about staff size, composition, and pay structures point to the need for greater disclosure. Even the most dedicated scholar or investigative reporter often cannot unearth important material on executive branch staffing or decision and policy processes. A more open system not only would facilitate this endeavor, but also might provide information that ultimately leads to improvements in executive staffing or to more reasonable expectations of presidential performance.

In this chapter we focus on the White House staff, just one part of the vast presidential advisory system. Within that group of aides, we examine some of the meaningful units and levels of analysis in an effort to identify key indicators for an institutional checkup. This presentation of the ideal and the reality of presidential staffing along two dimensions and from three perspectives provides a sense of the magnitude of this task and the related difficulty of identifying meaningful indicators of performance. Still, despite the inherent difficulties, evaluating the health of this critical component of governing may well prove valuable to future occupants, scholars, members of the media, and the interested public.

Notes

1. Such a recommendation is hardly novel. For example, Stephen Hess recommended to President-elect Jimmy Carter that "the White House organization should be freshly examined periodically—perhaps every six months (certainly once a year)," preferably by an "outsider." See memo, December 1, 1976, in Stephen Hess, *Organizing the Presidency*, 2d ed. (Brookings, 1988), pp. 253–55.

2. In the Clinton administration, for instance, the economic and domestic policy staffs were placed in the Office of Policy Development. Future checkups might well include the new Office of Homeland Security, which started with a staff of approximately one hundred. See Michael O'Hanlon and others, *Protecting the American Homeland: A Preliminary Analysis* (Brookings, 2002); Eric Pianin and Bradley Graham, "Ridge: Goal Isn't to Create Bureaucracy," *Washington Post*, October 4, 2001.

3. Bradley H. Patterson Jr., *The White House Staff: Inside the West Wing and Beyond* (Brookings, 2000), pp. 5ff, elaborates on the justifications for such an emphasis. None of the individuals in these offices has specific statutory duties, except for the president and vice president, and virtually all of them serve at the pleasure of the president. In addition, the papers and files of these offices are subject to the strictures of the Presidential Records Act, and a "strong tradition" exists militating against the appearance of these aides before congressional committees.

4. See Executive Order 8248 and Reorganization Plan of 1939.

5. John Hart, *The Presidential Branch: From Washington to Clinton* (Chatham House, 1995); Kathryn Dunn Tenpas and Matthew J. Dickinson, "Governing, Campaigning and Organizing the Presidency: An Electoral Connection?" *Political Science Quarterly*, vol. 112 (Spring 1997), p. 63.

6. Matthew J. Dickinson, *Bitter Harvest: FDR, Presidential Power and the Growth of the Executive Branch* (Cambridge University Press, 1997), p. 87.

7. Lyn Ragsdale, *Vital Statistics on the Presidency: From Washington to Clinton*, rev. ed. (Congressional Quarterly, 1998), p. 254.

8. The issue of staff size is vexing largely because of the difficulty of obtaining precise data. In addition, presidents since Gerald Ford have pledged to cut the size of their staffs in order to set a good example for the rest of the government. After having made this promise, they have frequently realized the significance of

their staffs and have often resorted to "creative accounting" to generate the perception of downsizing (for example, using detailees from the executive branch to assist with EOP operations and projects). A number of scholars have examined the issue of staff size, generating a variety of findings. For example, Hart, *The Presidential Branch*, pp. 112–25, provides four measures of the White House staff from 1939 to 1975, as well as staff totals reported under the White House Personnel Authorization-Employment Act of 1978. Ragsdale, *Vital Statistics on the Presidency*, pp. 264–68, relies on data taken from the *Statistical Abstract of the United States*, the *Budget of the United States*, and the Office of Personnel Management's *Federal Civilian Workforce Statistics*. Patterson, *The White House Staff*, pp. 345–48, bases the most recent calculation on numbers reported to Congress under a federal statute (P.L. 95-570) that requires the White House to report its staffing levels annually to Congress.

9. See, for example, Charles E. Walcott and Karen M. Hult, "White House Staff Size: Explanations and Implications," *Presidential Studies Quarterly*, vol. 29 (September 1999), esp. pp. 642–44 and figure 1.

10. One example has been the National Security Council staff. See, for example, Ivo H. Daalder, and I. M. Destler, "A New NSC for a New Administration," Policy Brief #68 (Brookings, November 2000) (www.brookings.edu/comm/policy_briefs/pb068/pb68.htm [November 27, 2000]). At least at the outset of the George W. Bush administration, however, Assistant to the President for National Security Affairs Condoleezza Rice reportedly cut the NSC staff "by 30%, to about 70 policy professionals." Moreover, "both legislative affairs and communications are now handled by the White House proper, while a small NSC press and speechwriting office works with much larger White House operations" (Ivo H. Daalder and I. M. Destler, "How Operational and Visible an NSC?" *Brookings*, February 23, 2001 [www.brook.edu/views/oped/daalder/20010223.htm; May 15, 2002]).

11. Patterson, *The White House Staff*, p. 1.

12. Hart, *The Presidential Branch*, p. 3.

13. See, for example, David Gergen, *Eyewitness to Power* (Simon and Schuster, 2000); George Stephanopoulos, *All Too Human* (Little, Brown, 1999); Edwin Meese, *With Reagan* (Regnery Gateway, 1992); Clark Clifford with Richard Holbrooke, *Counsel to the President* (Random House, 1991); Peggy Noonan, *What I Saw at the Revolution* (Ivy Books, 1990); and Harry McPherson, *A Political Education* (Little, Brown, 1972). Although not a formal member of the White House staff, political consultant Dick Morris, *Behind the Oval Office* (Renaissance Books, 1999), offers a unique perspective on the Clinton White House in the aftermath of the 1994 congressional elections.

14. See, for instance, Mary Anne Borrelli, Karen Hult, and Nancy Kassop, "The White House Counsel's Office," *Presidential Studies Quarterly*, vol. 31 (December 2001), pp. 561–84.

15. Through elected officials as well as via media reports, staff can be seen as responsive to citizens.

16. These two criteria need not be consistent with each other. Acceding to particular demands for information from congressional committees or journal-

ists, for example, may undermine the effectiveness of a senior aide in working with the president or with other advisers.

17. Rather clearly, views of "adequacy" may differ widely. *Whose* views of what is adequate are relevant. The likely demands and perceptions of particular actors (the president, members of the Washington community, and aides themselves) are considered later in the text.

18. For fuller examination of this point, see, for example, Hart, *The Presidential Branch*; and Walcott and Hult, "White House Staff Size."

19. See, for instance, John H. Trattner, *The 2000 Prune Book: How to Succeed in Washington's Top Jobs* (Brookings/Council for Excellence in Government, 2000), pp. 2–5; John P. Burke, *The Institutional Presidency: Organizing and Managing the White House from FDR to Clinton* (Johns Hopkins University Press, 2000), pp. 33–34.

20. For example, in a study of for-profit organizations, Daniel J. Koys found that employee turnover (along with employee satisfaction and "organizational citizenship" behavior) influenced organizational effectiveness (measured as profitability and customer satisfaction). See "The Effects of Employee Satisfaction, Organizational Citizenship Behavior, and Turnover on Organizational Effectiveness: A Unit Level, Longitudinal Study," *Personnel Psychology*, vol. 54, no. 1 (2001), pp. 101–14.

21. See, for example, Burke, *The Institutional Presidency*; John Helmer and Louis Maisel, "Analytical Problems in the Study of Presidential Advice: The Domestic Council Staff in Flux," *Presidential Studies Quarterly*, vol. 8 (Winter 1978), pp. 45–67.

22. See, for example, Ronald J. Burke, and Astrid M. Richardsen, "Psychological Burnout in Organizations: Research and Intervention," in Robert T. Golembiewski, ed., *Handbook of Organizational Behavior*, 2d rev. and exp. ed. (Marcel Dekker, 2001), p. 346.

23. Salary may well be an increasing problem, for both recruitment and retention, as individuals contend with rising living costs in the Washington, D.C., area. The Bureau of Labor Statistics, for instance, estimates that "Washington-area housing costs in 2000 were more than five times their level in 1969." See Gary Burtless, "How Much Is Enough? Setting Pay for Presidential Appointees," report commissioned by the Presidential Appointee Initiative, March 22, 2002, p. 8.

24. Trattner, *The 2000 Prune Book*, p. 3.

25. See, for example, Paul C. Light, *Thickening Government: Federal Hierarchy and the Diffusion of Accountability* (Brookings, 1995).

26. See, for example, the comments and expressions of "concern" in the reports of House and Senate appropriations committees on the Treasury, Postal Service, and General Government Appropriations Bill, FY 1997 (thomas.loc.gov [December 27, 2000]).

27. Our use of "transparent" is similar to that of Neal Finkelstein and others, although our emphasis is on the president's advisory system while theirs is on public policy. Finkelstein uses "transparent" to describe "those policies that are easily understood, where information about the policy is available, where ac-

countability is clear, and where citizens know what role they play in the implementation of policy." See Neal D. Finkelstein, ed., *Transparency in Public Policy: Great Britain and the United States* (St. Martin's, 2000), p. 1.

28. Robert T. Keller, "Cross-Functional Project Groups in Research and New Product Development: Diversity, Communications, Job Stress, and Outcomes," *Academy of Management Journal*, vol. 44 (June 2001), pp. 547–55, reports that, at least in cross-functional project groups, functional diversity improved "technical quality and scheduling and budgeting performance" but reduced "group cohesion."

29. Karen M. Hult, "Strengthening Presidential Decision-Making Capacity," *Presidential Studies Quarterly*, vol. 30 (March 2000), p. 29, emphasis added. Others who stress similar elements of procedural rationality include, for example, Burke, *The Institutional Presidency*; Daalder and Destler, "A New NSC for a New Administration"; I. M. Destler, *The National Economic Council: A Work in Progress* (Institute for International Economics, 1996); Kenneth L. Juster and Simon Lazarus, *Making Economic Policy: An Assessment of the National Economic Council* (Brookings, 1997); Karl E. Weick, Kathleen M. Sutcliffe, and David Obstfeld, "Organizing for High Reliability: Processes of Collective Mindfulness," in Robert I. Sutton and Barry M. Staw, eds., *Research in Organizational Behavior*, vol. 21 (JAI Press, 1999), p. 95.

30. Cf. Meena Bose, *Shaping and Signaling Presidential Policy: The National Security Decision-Making of Eisenhower and Kennedy* (Texas A&M University Press, 1998); Burke, *The Institutional Presidency*; Alexander L. George, *Presidential Decisionmaking in Foreign Policy: The Effective Use of Information and Advice* (Westview, 1980); Hult, "Strengthening Presidential Decision-Making Capacity."

31. See, for example, Hult, "Strengthening Presidential Decision-Making Capacity."

32. Such assessments are central, for example, to "stakeholder analysis" in policy evaluation.

33. Several of these elements are components of what has come to be labeled "burnout." Considerable research suggests that "emotional exhaustion" is a key component of burnout in work settings. Among the factors Burke and Richardsen report (in "Psychological Burnout in Organizations: Research and Intervention," pp. 343–44) as being related to emotional exhaustion are heavy workload, conflictual or hostile relationships with supervisors, "role ambiguity" ("the lack of clear, consistent information regarding the rights, duties, and responsibilities of the job and how these duties and responsibilities can best be performed"), and lack of control (where "control involves the perception of being able to influence decision-making in important aspects of the job"). See too Robert T. Golembiewski, Robert A. Boudreau, Robert F. Munzenrider, and Huaping Lao, "Global Burnout: A Worldwide Pandemic Explored by the Phase Model," *Monographs in Organizational Behavior and Industrial Relations*, vol. 21 (JAI Press 1996), pp. 216ff.

34. Interviews from the White House 2001 Project (funded by the Pew Charitable Trusts) are scheduled to be made available to scholars through the National

Archives sometime in late 2003. Other material from the project is available at whitehouse2001.org; in the June, September, and December 2001 issues of *Presidential Studies Quarterly*; and in Martha Joynt Kumar and Terry Sullivan, eds., *The White House World: Transitions, Organization, and Office Operations* (Texas A&M University Press, 2003).

35. Patterson, *The White House Staff*, p. 347.

36. Such problems are even more serious for presidential nominees who must be confirmed by the U.S. Senate. See, for example, Terry Sullivan, "In Full View: The Inquiry of Presidential Nominees," Report 15, White House 2001 Project, March 29, 2001 (whitehouse2001.org); Paul C. Light and Virginia Thomas, *The Merit and Reputation of an Administration: Presidential Appointees on the Appointments Process* (Presidential Appointees Initiative, 2000); G. Calvin Mackenzie, ed., *Innocent until Nominated: The Breakdown of the Presidential Appointments Process* (Brookings, 2001).

37. Examples include Anna L. Brownson, ed., *Federal Staff Directory/2*, 19th ed. (Staff Directories, Ltd., 1994); Peggie Rayhawk and Gary P. Osifchin, *The Almanac of the Executive Branch 1997–98* (Almanac Publishing, 1997); and *Carroll's Federal Directory* (Carroll Publishing, November/December, 2000).

38. As the Volcker Commission underscored, of course, "quality is an illusive term. Measuring it will always be difficult." See Volcker Commission Report (The Report of the National Commission on the Public Service), *Leadership for America: Rebuilding the Public Service* (Lexington Books, 1990), p. 139. Indeed, the General Accounting Office has noted that to evaluate employee quality, "one needs information on employee knowledge, skills, and ability, as well as data on individuals' attitudes, values, knowledge, skills, and ability, and on the match of the individual's capacities and the requirements of the job"; see Joel D. Aberbach and Bert A. Rockman, *In the Web of Politics: Three Decades of the Federal Executive* (Brookings, 2000), p. 54. Such data are unlikely to be widely available. See too George C. Edwards, "Why Not the Best? The Loyalty-Competence Trade-Off in Presidential Appointments," in Mackenzie, ed., *Innocent until Nominated*.

39. See Kathryn Dunn Tenpas and Stephen Hess, "The Bush White House: First Appraisals," *Presidential Studies Quarterly*, vol. 32 (September 2002), pp. 577–85. The authors use biographical material from successive "Decisionmaker" editions to identify and analyze incoming White House staffs.

40. See, for example, the listings of detailees by EOP unit in U.S. House of Representatives, "White House Personnel Authorization Act of 1978: To Review Transportation Expenditures under the Act," hearings before the Subcommittee on Human Resources of the Committee on Post Office and Civil Service, March 31; April 8, 9, 30; July 21, 1992 (Government Printing Office, Serial No. 102-46, 1993), pp. 40–42. Unfortunately, such reporting does not appear to occur or to be made public on a regular basis.

41. Matthew J. Dickinson and Kathryn Dunn Tenpas, "Explaining Increasing Turnover Rates among Presidential Advisors, 1929–1997," *Journal of Politics*, vol. 64 (May 2002), pp. 434–48.

42. Increasing turnover also may be a symptom of burnout among staffers; Burke and Richardsen, "Psychological Burnout in Organizations."

43. Alternatively, a cycle of "increasing effectiveness" would lead one to predict that aides' reported mistakes would *decrease* over the course of an administration. See Paul C. Light, *The President's Agenda: Domestic Policy Choice from Kennedy to Clinton,* 3d ed. (Johns Hopkins University Press, 1999).

44. Indeed, as we suggested earlier, the absence of access to senior officials or of information about formal procedures may contribute to burnout.

45. Possible sources include Ragsdale, *Vital Statistics on the Presidency*; Hart, *The Presidential Branch;* Walcott and Hult, "White House Staff Size"; annual reports responsive to the White House Personnel Authorization-Employment Act of 1978; monthly data on EOP units from "Employment and Trends," Federal Civilian Workforce Statistics, U.S. Office of Personnel Management. The OPM data are available electronically dating from November 1997. See, for example, table 2, "Comparison of Total Civilian Employment of the Federal Government by Branch, Agency, and Area as of June 2000 and July 2000" (www.opm.gov/feddata/etjuly00.pdf [December 27, 2000]). Among other things, the table reports the number of employees in the Executive Office of the President as well as in specific EOP subunits.

46. See, for example, Ragsdale, *Vital Statistics on the Presidency.*

47. For example, Dickinson, *Bitter Harvest*; Hult, "Strengthening Presidential Decision-Making Capacity"; Daniel E. Ponder, *Good Advice: Information and Policy Making in the White House* (Texas A&M University Press, 2000).

48. John Kessel, "The Structure of the Carter White House," *American Journal of Political Science*, vol. 27 (1983), pp. 431–63; John Kessel, "The Structure of the Reagan White House," *American Journal of Political Science*, vol. 28 (1984), pp. 231–58; Kessel, "White House Structure during Reagan's Second Term," in Paul Brace, Christine B. Harrington, and Gary King, eds., *The Presidency in American Politics* (New York University Press, 1989). Interviews with aides in the Carter and Reagan White Houses suggest both the value and the possibility of doing systematic, structured questioning of presidential staff. Kessel's emphasis, though, differed from that proposed here.

49. John P. Burke and Fred I. Greenstein, with the collaboration of Larry Berman and Richard Immerman, *How Presidents Test Reality: Decisions on Vietnam, 1954 and 1965* (Russell Sage, 1989); Alexander Moens, *Foreign Policy under Carter: Testing Multiple Advocacy Decision Making* (Westview, 1990); Ponder, *Good Advice.*

50. Dickinson and Tenpas, "Explaining Increasing Turnover Rates among Presidential Advisors."

51. The *U.S. Government Manual* is the most accessible source of individual-level data, but it has notable weaknesses. First, the listings only partially reflect the upper levels of staff appointees. Second, because submissions are not bound by strict standards, one administration's staff listing may be more (or less) inclusive than another, and a single administration's listings may vary over the course of the presidency. Third, the manual does not take into account midyear departures. Finally, beginning in the 1970s, the publication of the manual switched from a calendar year to a fiscal year basis.

FIVE

Measuring the Health of the Federal Public Service

PAUL C. LIGHT

Imagine for a moment the worst possible circumstances for an effective public service. At the top of the hierarchy we would argue that more leaders means more leadership, thereby encouraging presidents and career executives alike to create ever more layers in the effort to strengthen control. At the same time, we would tolerate high vacancy rates at the top, again deceiving ourselves that a 20 to 30 percent vacancy rate is a perfectly acceptable path to accountability.

At the middle and bottom of the hierarchy, we would limit training and development, arguing that mediocrity was just fine for government work. We would buffet government with efforts to make government work, changing philosophies of reform with little notice, never allowing the latest reform to take hold before switching direction. Although we might very well adjust pay to keep up with the private sector, we would set entry levels low enough to ensure that we could never recruit from the top of the class, rendering government an employer of last resort for employees who cannot land elsewhere. And, when it came time to downsize with the latest budget cuts, we would do so through attrition or voluntary buyouts, rarely asking which jobs and what kinds of employees should stay or go, choosing instead a kind of downsizing lottery in which the most talented employees are given the greatest incentives to leave.

Outside the hierarchy, we would create such hostility toward government that America's best and brightest college students would never consider a public service career. We would denigrate government in our political campaigns, belittling what government does well while celebrating scandal. We would multiply that cynicism through a campaign finance system that, while completely legal, created the unrelenting appearance of influence peddling. We would encourage presidents to use the perquisites of office to generate campaign contributions but create "no controlling legal authority" that might otherwise limit their behavior.

The problem, of course, is that this is not just an imagined worst case, but the way things really are. In the public service in the early 2000s, many of the prevailing conditions are the exact opposite of what might be preferred for high performance. The hierarchy governing the federal government's 1.7 million employees and its 5.6 million contract and grant employees is too tall, vacancies at the top are too numerous, training budgets are too low, public cynicism is too high, government appears to be eliminating jobs with little consideration about what should stay and go, and young people are still turned off and tuned out to public service careers.[1] In many ways, the federal government could not have been better designed for ineffectiveness.

A Healthy Public Service

Just because government has considerable reason to be ineffective does not mean it actually is ineffective. The thickening of the hierarchy, vacancy rates, and public cynicism are no doubt dispiriting to those in the public service, but they may not be determinative of actual performance. Moreover, as the first Volcker Commission (formally, the National Commission on the Public Service) most certainly believed, what may matter most to public service performance is the deep commitment to making a difference that so many public servants bring to their work.

Thus it may be best to view the conditions of ineffectiveness as potential drags on performance, but not as pure determinants. Certainly, the thickness of the hierarchy contributes to poor performance at times, reducing the clarity of direction moving down the hierarchy and diffusing accountability. That appears to have been the case, for example, at the Internal Revenue Service, where the creation of new management layers rendered no one ultimately accountable for what went right or wrong on the front lines. Absent a clear chain of command between the top and bottom of the IRS, district managers could invent just about any scheme they wanted to monitor their employees, while rogue revenue agents could easily persuade themselves that no one at the top would ever catch on.[2]

The Volcker Assessment

Nevertheless, even as one might criticize such thickening, the changing shape of the federal hierarchy may be far less important to underlying performance than, say, clarity of the statutes that describe what the front line is to do or the ability to recruit highly motivated civil servants. The question is not what is offensive for daily life in the public service, but what affects the outcomes of government. In this regard, I believe the 1988 National Commission on the Public Service chaired by Paul Volcker was right on target in articulating three major sources of effectiveness: leadership, capacity, and incentives for performance.

Start with leadership, where the commission made its case for the conditions of effectiveness by arguing that no president can be effective alone. He or she must rely on a sizable number of top officials—leaders in their own right—to ensure the quality and effectiveness of government. These men and women—presidential appointees, senior career executives, and personal and confidential assistants—implement the president's agenda, hire and promote the key staff, draft the budget, enforce the laws, try to anticipate problems and get the facts, and motivate the civil service.[3]

The commission said that the quality of senior leadership mattered in two ways. First, quality matters when the senior leadership is asked to execute the president's agenda and discharge the obligations of office as specified in the Constitution, governing statutes, and executive orders. Second, it matters in signaling those inside government and the public writ large regarding the president's commitment to the highest levels of competence and conduct. Government cannot rebuild the public's trust, for example, if its leaders engage in conduct that creates the appearance of a conflict of interest. Nor can government be particularly well executed if the president's senior leadership is of such mediocre quality that it is incapable of doing its job.

The commission saw these two issues as intimately linked to a broad restoration of trust in government. "America must have a public service that can value the lessons of experience and appreciate the requirements for change; a public service that both responds to political leadership and respects the law; a public service with the professional skills and the ethical sensitivity America deserves."[4] In turn, increased public trust would restore a sense of pride in public service to those who choose to serve, which would help draw talented individuals back to government.

A similar argument prevailed in the commission's analysis of governmental capacity. Here, the commission argued that a deep talent pool was essential given the need for creative solutions to the nation's problems. "Young Americans have always been a source of creative energy for government," the commission argued. "Their natural enthusiasm and willingness to question the status quo are important counterweights to the inertia that can set in as an agency and its work force age."[5] Just as the quality of senior leadership threatened the performance and oversight of government, the commission worried that an erosion of the talent pool would weaken government's ability to honor its promises, whether at the Social Security Administration or at federal Air Traffic Control. In recommending a more aggressive recruitment program for women and minorities, the commission also endorsed the need for greater representation as part of basic democratic accountability.

The commission's recommendations on leadership and recruitment are well anchored, therefore, in a capacity-based model of accountability.[6] Simply stated, government will do the right thing if it is given the leadership and talent to do so. Unlike compliance-based accountability, which seeks effectiveness through the deterrence created by audits and investigations, capacity-based accountability seeks effectiveness by providing the leadership and tools needed before action occurs. Presidents and their chief lieutenants are seen not as supervisors and discipliners, but as advocates and stewards for the public service over the long term.

Although the commission clearly believed in restoring the basic capacity of government and rejected the principles of compliance-based accountability (as did President Richard Nixon and Vice President Al Gore, both of whom characterized the problem in federal management as good people trapped in rule-bound systems), it was not ready to place all its faith in a well-led, well-trained work force. It also endorsed the notion that government should demand higher performance standards from its employees. Yes, those in the public service should be paid a competitive salary, and yes, they should be celebrated for their commitment to the greater good. But the Volcker Commission also believed that government needed to develop and strengthen what it called a "culture of performance."

Although the commission did not anticipate the movement toward performance-based accountability in statutes such as the 1993 Government Performance and Results Act, it did recommend a quid pro quo in pushing for higher pay by encouraging "the President and Congress to use their respective budget and oversight authorities to monitor closely progress toward improving standards of employee performance, while eliminating duplication of services and unnecessary layers of government."[7] One can argue that the Results Act, as it is now called, is just such a tool for monitoring progress toward higher standards of employee performance through an annual planning process. Through such systems, pay and other key inputs such as staffing and budget would be linked to actual performance, creating incentives for effective performance.

Measures of Effectiveness

The Volcker Commission used a host of measures to assess the conditions of effectiveness described above. Some were little more than collected anecdotes; others involved surveys conducted by the commission itself. In all, the commission cited fifty-two measures in its final report to support its evaluation of the state of the public service.

The Volcker Commission asked several questions in creating an overall portrait of the senior civil service: Would senior executives recommend a job in government to their own children? (Fewer than half said they would.) Does the bonus system provide strong incentives to meet job objectives? (Fifty-seven percent of federal personnel officers said no.) Do senior executives see any link between actual performance and the bonus pay system? (Seventy-six percent of IRS executives said no.) And would senior executives take a job outside government if a suitable post opened up? (Over half said they would take it.) The commission also drew upon surveys of Presidential Management Interns (three-quarters of whom said they intended to leave government within ten years), Office of Personnel Management employees (44 percent of whom said morale was low or very low, and two-thirds of whom said turnover of experienced staff had weakened their ability to accomplish their goals), and anecdotes from around the federal agencies.

It is one thing to argue that recruitment has become more difficult, quite another to conclude that effectiveness has been compromised. It is not necessary, for example, to have a huge pool of talented young people to find the needed talent. The best the Volcker Commission could do, therefore, was draw broad portraits of the state of being needed for effectiveness. "If I as a CEO were to say that I have loafers, laggards and petty thieves working for me," said commission member and former secretary of defense Frank Carlucci, "one could hardly expect my people to perform. Nor would such talk inspire customer confidence; indeed they would wonder about us as a company and about me as a CEO."[8]

Bluntly put, there is little or no firm evidence of a link between any of the broad conditions of effectiveness described above and actual performance. Part of the problem is that public administration scholars have not made much progress in either defining or measuring any links. We have some strong hunches about what relates to what—for example, that organizational structure matters somehow to performance—but not much more than hunches. The theory is reasonably strong, but the measurement weak. Part of the problem is that government has not done very well at measuring the dependent variable of performance, as witnessed in the uneven implementation of the Results Act. Much as one might hope for precise measures of performance against which to test the impact of different conditions of effectiveness, such measures simply do not exist. Though less than ideal, the Volcker measures constitute one of the few available baselines against which to measure the condition of the public service. And, as the following pages suggest, that condition has worsened since. Despite occasional bright spots, such as an increase in morale among civil servants and their somewhat greater willingness to recommend careers in government to young people, the basic components of an effective public service are still in decline at this writing in 2003, some ten years post–Volcker Commission.

The Health of the Public Service Today

There are two ways of assembling the data on the state of the public service at any given point in time. The first is to look at objective indicators of health at different levels of the work force. It could well be, for example, that the federal service is healthy at the middle levels or at the top, but in trouble at the entry level. The second is to look at a set of subjective indicators involving perceptions of federal workers themselves. In a sense, health is in the eye of the beholder.

There are also two ways to generate data on the state of the public service. The first is to take a snapshot of conditions of effectiveness at a single point in time, thereby generating a static image of health. The second is to take multiple measures of health over time, using panel surveys and other time-based measures to establish trend lines of increasing or decreasing health.

The following pages combine these approaches in two different diagnostic efforts. The first examines a mix of static objective evidence at different levels of the public service; the second examines subjective evidence drawn from opinion surveys of federal employees and the public, sorted by a general template describing five characteristics of a healthy public service.

Measuring Health by Work-Force Level

The current conversation about civil service reform focuses almost exclusively on strengthening entry-level recruitment, in part because entry-level recruitment is arguably the easiest to fix. However, research suggests that recruitment reform will only move the problem from the entry level to the early retention level. Without a systematic top-to-bottom approach, life in the federal public service will not improve for long. Consider the following trends culled from recent research on the state of the public service by level.

AT THE EARLY-CAREER LEVEL.   According to an unpublished survey of 1,015 college students by the Center for Public Service, only 13 percent of liberal arts graduates in the class of 2002 said they had given serious consideration to working for the federal government. Business came in first at 31 percent, state and local government second at 30 percent, and the nonprofit sector third at 18 percent. Young Americans increasingly believe that the most rewarding public service work is not in the federal government, but in nonprofit agencies, state and local governments, and private firms that deliver goods and services on the federal government's behalf. According to the survey, top students do not believe the federal government provides the challenging and interesting work they desire. Although entry-level pay and benefits must meet minimum labor-market expectations, talented Americans emphasize the nature of the work.

There is also good evidence that the federal government is increasingly unable to fill jobs from the outside. According to the National Academy of Public Administration's Center for Human Resources Management, 42 percent of the federal government's entry-level jobs during the 1990s were filled by someone already on the federal payroll. Parents and teachers remain a neglected focus in efforts to improve the image of federal careers. Asked which careers offered the greatest potential for their children in a June 2000 Harris Poll, just 11 percent of parents and 25 percent of teachers said that government was a promising career.[9]

Vacancies throughout the federal government are likely to expand rapidly in the early twenty-first century. By 2005, more than half the federal work force will be eligible to retire.[10] Hiring freezes and attrition-based downsizing have left an indelible mark on the age structure of the federal work force. In the year 2000, the average federal employee was 45 years old, 32 percent were eligible for retirement by 2004, and another 21 percent will be eligible for early retirement.[11] Preliminary data suggest the presence of a growing gap between the average age of the federal government's entry-level work force and its baby-boom middle and upper levels. The resulting "bathtub" or "valley" means that there are fewer potential leaders for future middle- and senior-level positions.

Although the size of the contract work force (in products and services) is down since the end of the cold war, the number of service contract workers appears to be rising as agencies put more and more jobs up for competition. The growth is particularly noticeable in hard-to-recruit areas such as information technology, where 80 percent of federal work is now done by contractors, and in management analysis and consulting.

AT THE MIDDLE-CAREER LEVEL.   The federal government continues to have great difficulty retaining talented employees over the longer term. Only 30 percent of federal employees hired in the early 1980s are still in government in 2003, for example. It is not clear, however, that the right 30 percent stayed. Unlike the military, which uses an up-or-out system, retention is more a product of accident than of intent. Only 45 percent of the federal employees and supervisors interviewed by the Merit Systems Protection Board in 2001 said their supervisors promoted the most qualified person when jobs were open.[12]

There is little access to middle-level employment from outside of government. According to a study by the Partnership for Public Service, outside candidates were unable to apply for nearly half the vacant middle-level civil service jobs in 2001.[13] Even when they did apply, the odds were against them. In 2000, for example, only 13 percent of mid-career hires were candidates who did not already hold federal jobs.[14]

AT THE SENIOR CAREER LEVEL.   Retirements at the senior levels of government will soon increase dramatically. By 2005, over 70 percent of senior executives will be eligible for retirement.[15] Although job satisfaction, morale, sense of purpose, and perceived access to resources were all very high among the senior executives interviewed for the Center for Public Service "State of the Public Service" report, these senior executives also expressed significant dissatisfaction with their salaries and their organization's access to enough training and employees to do their jobs well.[16]

Pay gaps are also increasing. Using data collected from private firms, the Congressional Budget Office reported significant gaps in 1999 between the salaries and benefits of senior executives and private employees at large, medium-sized, and small private firms, and rough parity with most officers at large nonprofits. Senior federal executives, career and political, made roughly one-tenth as much as chief financial officers at America's largest private firms in 1999, one-sixteenth as much as chief operating officers, and one-thirty-fifth as much as chief executive officers.

Senior executives report that promotion into the Senior Executive Service (SES) has become a career capstone, not a highly prestigious step upward. The Senior Executive Service was created in 1978 in part to give the president greater flexibility in redeploying employees at the top of government and in part to create a more prestigious capstone for civil service careers. However, the SES has never quite become the highly mobile, generalist work force that its designers hoped to create. According to a 1992 survey, less than a quarter of SES members said they had served in an agency other than the one in which they were originally hired.

AT THE PRESIDENTIAL APPOINTEE LEVEL.   Past appointees report a growing host of problems in the appointments process. Analyses of experiences in the Reagan, first Bush, and Clinton administrations suggest that (1) delays in staffing new administrations are increasing, (2) confusion and embarrassment are rising, (3) all stages of the process take longer than necessary, (4) both branches contribute to the problem, and (5) the process increasingly favors candidates with prior government experience who already live in Washington.

According to research by the Brookings Institution's Presidential Appointee Initiative, delays continue to rise at both ends of Pennsylvania Avenue. As of October 31, 2001, almost two months after the attacks on New York City and Washington, more than one out of five senior positions involved in the war on terrorism and homeland security were still vacant. As of August 1, 2002, the Bush administration had become the slowest in modern history to fill its top jobs. The average number of days from inauguration to confirmation for President Bush's first-year appointees was 181. This represents a dramatic increase from President Reagan's inaugural year average of 142 days and a slight increase over President Clinton's average of 174 days.

Although the desire to serve remains strong among America's civic leaders, fears of the process are a significant predictor of a declining unwillingness to accept a position if offered. Most of the 580 *Fortune 500* executives, university and college presidents, nonprofit executives, state and local government officials, think tank scholars, and top lobbyists interviewed for the Presidential Appointee Initiative viewed the current process as unfair, confusing, and embarrassing, and were more likely than those who had actually served as appointees in the past to see the process as an ordeal at both ends of Pennsylvania Avenue.

Pay compression has eroded interest in government service among potential presidential and judicial appointees and has weakened retention. Federal district court judges make barely as much as junior associates at America's largest law firms, while the nation's corporate chief executives make ninety-three times as much on average as members of Congress, and presidential appointees trail in virtually every comparison. The gaps are particularly severe in the federal judiciary. Federal district and circuit court judges have lost almost 25 percent in purchasing power to inflation since 1969, while Supreme Court justices have lost 38 percent (more than half of that since 1993).[17]

Measuring Health over Time

Static measures of the health of institutions are only the first step in creating a meaningful portrait of institutional capacity. One must also track key indicators over time, whether through objective measures such as turnover, recruitment, and career advancement, or subjective measures such as morale, job satisfaction, and sense of purpose. As the previous discussion suggests, there has been a general decay in the objective measures of the health of the federal public service over the past fifteen years. And as the following discussion suggests, that decline has created a distinctly negative set of attitudes among federal workers themselves.

The evidence comes from a unique pre– and post–September 11 survey of the same random sample of federal government employees. The first telephone survey of 1,051 randomly selected employees was taken from February to June 2001, and the second survey of 673 of the same employees was taken from March to May 2002. Both surveys were conducted by Princeton Survey Research Associates on behalf of the Brookings Institution's Center for Public Service. Interviewed at home, not on the job, these employees were given a rare chance to be completely candid about life in their organizations.[18]

According to the surveys, federal employees became less satisfied with their jobs over the year. They also reported lower morale among their coworkers, continuing difficulty securing the resources they need to do their jobs, growing uncertainty regarding the link between their work and the mission of their agencies, and less trust in their own organizations to do the right thing. Although some of these trends were small in percentage terms, they were statistically significant nonetheless, and definitely in the wrong direction for a healthy public service.[19]

All federal employees were not equally dissatisfied, however. In 2002, Defense Department employees were more likely to say they were given a chance to do the things they do best than they were in 2001, and they reported improved performance among their peers. They were also more likely to say that their organizations provided enough employees to do their jobs well, and were much more likely to feel a greater sense of purpose in 2002 than their non–Defense Department peers.[20]

Yet even Defense employees said morale had fallen among their coworkers over the previous year, as had the chance to accomplish something worthwhile at work. They were also less likely to say that they contributed a great deal to their organization's mission, and were more likely than their non-Defense colleagues to say that their organizations do not always provide enough training to do their jobs well.

One thing that increased among Defense and non-Defense employees alike is the sense that there are too many layers of managers in their organizations. If we assume that this perceived layering is a symptom of red tape and paperwork, federal employees were feeling more burdened by needless interference and managerial nitpicking. The two surveys do not necessarily create a portrait of despair. One can easily argue that frustration is up because federal employees have become more aware of the bureaucratic barriers to performance in this post–September 11 world. Hence the perceived increase in the number of layers.

One can also argue that perceived morale is down because federal employees wanted to do more to help the nation. As one federal employee tried to explain the decline in morale, "There are so many different factors that could contribute to that feeling. There was this neglect of people and facilities. Then we find out we have a major crisis in the country and we're really not prepared to deal with it. We did not invest in our infrastructure and in our people. . . . Now people are rediscovering the weaknesses that we have, which all of us knew all along, but no one was listening."[21]

One factor that does not explain the change is the economic recession and nascent recovery. To the contrary, private sector employees interviewed pre– and post–September 11 reported higher morale among their coworkers, increased job satisfaction, greater access to enough employees to do the job well, and more pride in where they work.[22]

A healthy public service has five characteristics. It is motivated by the chance to accomplish something worthwhile on behalf of the country, recruited from the top of the labor market, given the resources and organizational capacity to succeed, rewarded for a job well done, and respected by the people and leaders it serves. By all five measures, the federal service lost ground after September 11:

—*Federal employees were less likely to go to work in 2002 for the chance to accomplish something worthwhile.* The number of federal employees who said they went to work solely for the paycheck increased from 31 percent in 2001 to 41 percent in 2002. At the same time, the number who said they were very satisfied with the opportunity to accomplish something worthwhile fell 8 percentage points to 39 percent, and the number who felt that they personally contribute a great deal to their organization's mission fell by 11 percentage points to 45 percent.

—*The federal government was less likely to offer the kind of challenging work in 2002 that attracts the top of the labor market.* The number of federal employees who saw their work as boring did not change after September 11, but the number who saw their work as a dead end with no future went up by 3 percent governmentwide, and by 7 percent among non-Defense employees. Among Defense Department employees, the number who strongly agreed that they are given the chance to do the things they do best increased by 14 percentage points to 59 percent over the year, even as the number of non-Defense employees who strongly agreed fell by 6 percentage points to 38 percent.

—*The federal government continued to under-resource its employees.* Although federal employees reported high levels of continued access to information and technological equipment over the previous year, 40 percent said that their organizations only sometimes or rarely provided access to enough training to do their jobs well, and 56 percent reported that their organizations sometimes or rarely provided enough employees to do their jobs well. Although Defense employees reported a significant gain in adequate staffing over the year, they also reported a significant decline in access to training. Regardless of their agency, federal employees were significantly more likely to complain that there are too many layers between the top and bottom of their agencies.

—*The federal government continued to have difficulty rewarding a job well done.* Federal employees estimated that 22 percent of their peers were not performing their jobs in 2001 and in 2002. Asked to evaluate their organizations, they were less likely in 2002 to say their organizations were doing a good job either running their programs and services or helping people. Just 34 percent said their organization was very good at running its programs and services in 2002, compared to 40 percent in 2001. Although almost half of federal employees were very proud to tell their families and friends that they work for the government, the number who said they always trust their organization to do the right thing remained statistically unchanged at just 21 percent in 2002 and 23 percent in 2001.

—*The federal work force did not have the confidence and respect of the people it serves.* According to successive surveys by Princeton Survey Research Associates on behalf of the Center for Public Service, Americans continued to have doubts about the motivation and performance of federal employees.[23] Americans remained convinced that most federal employees are motivated primarily by the job security (70 percent pre–September 11 versus 71 percent in May 2002), salary and benefits (68 percent pre–September 11 versus 71 percent in 2002), and having a secure paycheck (68 percent pre–September 11 versus 69 percent in 2002). According to a May 2002 public opinion survey, Americans estimated that 42 percent of federal employees do not do their jobs well; a month later the number had increased to 48 percent.

Given these trends, perhaps it is no surprise that employee job satisfaction declined by 6 percentage points over the year: 49 percent said they were very satisfied in 2001, 43 percent in 2002. Nor is it surprising perhaps that federal employees sensed a general decline in morale among their peers: 58 percent of federal employees rated morale among their coworkers as very or somewhat high in 2001; 53 percent did so in 2002.

Not all the indicators are negative, however. The number of federal employees who said they accomplish something worthwhile at work remained virtually unchanged at 93 percent "yes," while 70 percent said they would rather work for government if given a choice of sectors.

Moreover, as noted earlier, some of these trends appear to be related to heightened concerns about barriers to high performance. Employees who do not have adequate training cannot be expected to feel highly confident that they accomplish something worthwhile at work, while employees who are buried under layers of supervision can hardly feel confident that they are personally contributing to their organization's mission.

Nevertheless, Congress and the president should be troubled by the fact that so many federal employees cannot easily describe how their job contributes to the mission of their organization, or that so few have confidence in their organizations to do the right thing. Moreover, at a time when the flow of information has become *the* issue of the day, Americans can hardly be reassured that so many federal employees see so many layers between the top and bottom of their agencies. If the federal public service is to meet public expectations at this crucial moment in history, it must stay focused on its mission and be given the tools to succeed. Both are question marks today.

Motivation

Americans go to work for many reasons: to pay the bills, see friends, use their talents, help people, and save for retirement, among others. But a healthy public service should be motivated first and foremost by the chance to accomplish something worthwhile for the community and country. Although pay, benefits, the opportunity to repay college loans, and job security are important assets in recruiting and retaining talented public servants, the government cannot succeed unless its work force cares about something more than the paycheck.

Unfortunately, the surveys suggest that federal employees may be paying more attention to the paycheck than to the chance to serve their country. Consider their answers to the simple open-ended question, "Why do you come to work every day?"[24]

—Forty-one percent of the employees focused solely on the paycheck, up from 31 percent in 2001. Among the common answers were "to pay the bills," "money," "it's my paycheck," "they pay me," "the salary and benefits," "my pocketbook tells me I still need to work," "to survive," "because I have to eat and live," "the kids," "my wife makes me and I have to make a living," "once in a while I enjoy it, but I need the money to pay the bills," and "show me the money."

—Twenty-eight percent of the employees focused solely on personal interest and satisfaction, down slightly from 2001. Among the common answers were "it's interesting and challenging," "I go to work to have fun," "what we bring to the government is value added," "love the job," "I think I'm accomplishing something here," "just for the challenges of new technologies to work with," "it's interesting, valuable work," "because I get the opportunity to learn," "accomplishment," "never a dull moment," and "because I enjoy getting up and going to work."

—Ten percent of the employees focused solely on the work ethic, down slightly from 2001. Among the common answers were "that's life," "I am from the old school that just goes to work," "I have so much to do and have a lot of people counting on me," and "it's my job."

—Seven percent of the employees responded with a combination of compensation and personal interest or satisfaction, essentially unchanged from 2001.

—Only 4 percent of the employees talked about the public good, down slightly from 2001. Among the common answers were "I go because I really feel like I am contributing a lot and help people immediately," "defending the country," "my job has a great impact on my community and country," "because I work for the veterans and care about them," "I believe in the mission of my agency," "the work since 9/11 is very important," and "to serve the people of the United States."

Although Defense employees were somewhat less likely than their non-Defense peers to focus on the paycheck (37 percent in 2001 versus 42 percent in 2002), the nation deserves better from both work forces. Simply put, too many government employees go to work for the wrong reason.

It is not comforting that private employees were even more likely to focus solely on the paycheck as a reason to go to work. Federal employees may be merely catching up to their private sector brethren in becoming more "businesslike," but they are in anything but a private business. Federal jobs call for a commitment to the public good. They may be frustrated by the lack of resources, worried about their personal safety, even angered by the president's decision to offer civilians a smaller pay increase than uniformed military personnel in 2002, but that is no excuse for these findings. Many federal employees need to take a hard look in the mirror. If they are going to work for the paycheck, they should get out. The nation needs a greater commitment from federal employees.

Federal employees need more than a harsh scolding, however. They also deserve the resources to do their jobs well. It may be no surprise that so many federal employees go to work for the paycheck. In far too many agencies, that is all they can go to work for.

THE SEPTEMBER 11 EFFECT.   The 2002 survey also clearly shows that federal employees were affected by September 11. Some federal employees

Table 5-1.   *Federal Employees' Sense of Purpose, Post–September 11*
Percent

Since September 11, do people you work with have more of a sense of purpose?	Governmentwide	Defense	Non-Defense
More	42	63	35
Less	1	0	1
Same	57	37	63

Note: N = 673 governmentwide (174 Defense, 499 non-Defense); interviews were conducted February–June 2001 and March–May 2002.

are still worried about their own safety. "You never know when the other shoe is going to fall," said one. "Everybody figures they're some kind of target. I don't know whether that's realistic or not, but it affects your morale for getting up and going to work in the morning." Others feel greater pride and urgency in their work.

Asked whether the people they work with have more or less sense of purpose since September 11, 42 percent of federal employees said "more," 1 percent said "less," and 57 percent said the "same." But the sense of purpose is not evenly distributed across the federal agencies. As table 5-1 shows, Defense Department employees are much more likely to feel a greater sense of duty post-September 11 than their non-Defense peers. In fact, the contrast is extreme.

Federal employees can hardly feel a greater sense of purpose post–September 11 if they cannot describe the mission of their agencies or how their own work contributes to that mission. "Maybe it's a lack of understanding of how important their jobs are," one federal employee said in trying to explain the finding. "Maybe their superiors or their agencies overall just don't tell them why they have to do these things. They're simply told 'You have to do this,' but they're not told why or what will be done with the work produced once they're finished with it."

The two surveys provide some confirming evidence of that speculation. Between 2001 and 2002, the number of federal employees who could very easily describe how their job contributes to their organization's mission fell by 4 percentage points governmentwide, 7 percentage points among non-Defense employees, and 3 percent among Defense employees. At the same time, the number who said that they personally contribute a great deal to accomplishing their organization's mission dropped 11 percentage points governmentwide, 12 percentage points among non-Defense employees, and 9 percentage points among Defense employees.

Table 5-2.   *Federal Employees' Views of the Job, Post–September 11*
Percent

How has job changed since September 11?	Governmentwide	Defense	Non-Defense
More difficult	27	31	25
More stressful	37	46	34
More rewarding	19	30	15
More challenging	31	45	26

Note: N = 673 governmentwide (174 Defense, 499 non-Defense); interviews conducted February–June 2001 and March–May 2002.

DEFENSE VERSUS NON-DEFENSE.   Defense and non-Defense employees may have come to the same conclusions about their ability to make a difference for very different reasons. As table 5-2 shows, Defense employees not only said they feel a greater sense of purpose since September 11; they were also more likely to say that their jobs have become more difficult, stressful, rewarding, and challenging. The good news is that Defense employees appear to know the mission very well; the bad news is that they view their jobs as more difficult and stressful than they used to. The result appears to be a dissatisfaction, perhaps healthy, among Defense employees regarding their individual ability to meet expectations.

This schism between the Defense and non-Defense work forces has implications for Congress and the president. If a healthy public service comes to work for the right reasons and knows how it will measure its success, the non-Defense work force needs more clarity regarding how their jobs matter in the post–September 11 world.

Recruitment

A healthy public service not only recruits aggressively; it also provides the kind of jobs that today's talent pool wants. Study after study shows that young Americans value interesting, challenging work above all else. Although employers have to offer competitive pay and help with college debt, talented recruits are saying, "Show us the work."

Unfortunately, federal work has not been showing well lately. Many federal employees report that their jobs simply do not provide the challenge they seek. Consider the following findings from the federal and private employee surveys.

—Private sector employees were more likely than public sector employees to say that their organization encourages them to take risks a great deal or fair amount of the time (a 9 percentage point difference).

—Private sector employees were more likely to strongly agree that they are given the chance to do the things they do best (an 11 percentage point difference).

—Private sector employees were less likely to say their jobs were a dead end with no future (an 8 percentage point difference).

—Private sector employees were more likely to be very satisfied with the public respect they receive for their work (a 12 percentage point difference).

—Private sector employees were more likely be very proud to tell friends and neighbors what organization they worked for (an 11 percentage point difference).

—Private sector employees were more likely to say they could describe how their job contributes to the mission of their organizations (a 10 percentage point difference).

—Finally, private sector employees were significantly more likely to report higher morale among their co-workers (an 18 percentage point difference).

At least in 2002, many federal employees would have been reluctant to recommend a job in their agencies. The number of federal employees who said they were very satisfied with their job overall declined seven points over the year, dropping to 43 percent, while the number who were very satisfied with the opportunity to accomplish something worthwhile declined by 9 percent, from 47 percent in 2001 to 39 percent in 2002. The only area in which federal employees reported higher satisfaction was job security, where the number who were very satisfied grew by 5 percent, from 66 percent very satisfied in 2001 to 71 percent in 2002. But that is hardly a sales advantage to college seniors who expect to stay a few years in a job and move on.

As earlier surveys found, Defense employees have a very different take on life in their agencies. The number of Defense employees who strongly agreed they have the chance to do the things they do best rose by 14 percent between 2001 and 2002, from 45 to 59 percent. During the same period, the number of non-Defense employees who said their jobs also gave them the chance to do the things they do best fell by 6 percent, from 44 to 38 percent.

The Defense work force is not without problems, however. Defense employees reported roughly the same decline in morale as their non-Defense peers (down 5 percent among the former and 4 percent among the latter), and a similar decline in satisfaction with the opportunity to accomplish something worthwhile.

Table 5-3.   *Impact of Post–September 11 Job Changes*
Nature of the statistical relationship

| | Change in job | | | |
Impact	More rewarding	More challenging	More difficult	More stressful
Higher morale among co-workers	Defense: + Non-Defense: +++	Defense: ++++ Non-Defense: 0	Defense: +++ Non-Defense: 0	Defense: 0 Non-Defense: 0
Greater satisfaction with the opportunity to accomplish something worthwhile	Defense: ++++ Non-Defense: ++++	Defense: ++++ Non-Defense: ++	Defense: +++ Non-Defense: ++	Defense: ++++ Non-Defense: +

Note: + means a correlation that is statistically significant at least at the 0.15 level, ++ at least at the .10 level, +++ at least at the .05 level, and ++++ at least at the .009 level; 0 means no statistically significant relationship. There were no negative correlations in this analysis. The more pluses, the stronger the relationship.

The decline in morale and in the perceived opportunity to accomplish something worthwhile appear to be closely related to September 11. It is no surprise that employees who said their jobs had become more rewarding or fulfilling since September 11 might perceive higher morale and greater opportunities to accomplish something worthwhile among their peers. The link is easy to make. But as table 5-3 shows, Defense employees also seemed to thrive on more stressful and difficult jobs. Perceived morale at Defense went up among employees who said their jobs had become more difficult after September 11, while the perceived opportunity to accomplish something worthwhile went up among employees who said that their jobs had become both more difficult and more stressful.

It is one thing to link rewarding, challenging jobs to morale and the opportunity to accomplish something worthwhile, and quite another to link difficult, stressful jobs to that opportunity. Yet Defense employees responded to every type of work, be it tough or fulfilling, challenging or stressful. As table 5-3 shows, so did many non-Defense employees, albeit to a less significant degree.

Resources

A healthy public service does not just recruit talented employees; it gives those employees the resources to succeed. Even as the Office of Personnel Management continues the long-overdue task of streamlining the federal hiring process, Congress and the president must make sure that employees have the resources and opportunity to succeed. "You can only ask for superhuman effort for so long," said one federal employee. "Federal employees have been doing it for so long, it's just wearing on them. I'm seeing more squabbles among co-workers and specialists. It's just that everybody doesn't have enough time to get their work done."

The proof is in the two surveys where significant numbers of federal employees reported continued problems getting access to the tools they need. Although one can argue that the federal government gives its employees enough information and technological equipment to succeed, especially in comparison with the private sector, many federal employees report difficulty with training and staffing. Many employees, private and public, complain about having too much work to do or not enough employees. But federal perceptions on these two resources are well above the levels found in the private sector:

—Forty percent of federal employees reported that their organizations only sometimes or rarely provided the training to do their jobs well in 2002; only 30 percent of private employees said the same thing.

—Fifty-six percent of federal employees reported that their organizations only sometimes or rarely provided enough employees to do their jobs well in 2002; just 36 percent of private employees said the same was true of their employers.

Some of the complaints about staffing shortages may be a defensive response to the Bush administration's "competitive sourcing" initiative, which will eventually require federal agencies to put 500,000 jobs up for bid from the private sector. "There's a lot of talk about privatization in government," one employee answered when asked why so many federal workers do not trust their organizations. "I think that makes people leery about government."

But many of the complaints may be rooted in a steady decline in the number of federal employees on the traditional front lines. As table 5-4 shows, the federal hierarchy continues its journey from a traditional bureaucratic pyramid, with more employees at the bottom than in the middle, to an inverted pyramid, with more employees in the middle than at the bottom. The old bureaucratic pyramid has not disappeared, however. Rather, the bottom is increasingly filled with contract employees who do the front-line work once done by the federal work force. The federal government is becoming an organization of managers, policymakers, inspectors, and contract officers.

Table 5-4.   *The Changing Federal Hierarchy, 1983–2001*
Full-time permanent civil service positions

Measure	1983	1987	1992	1997	2001
Total	2,009,000	2,040,000	2,106,000	1,778,000	1,675,000
General Schedule (GS) 1–10	783,000	797,000	767,000	594,000	535,000
GS 11–15	487,000	531,000	645,000	638,000	628,000
GS 11–15 managers and supervisors	125,000	137,000	160,000	126,000	119,000

Source: Analysis of data provided through the Central Personnel Data File, U.S. Office of Personnel Management, May 2001.

Some of the cuts involved obsolete jobs such as clerk-typist, but many were the result of hiring freezes instituted in the 1990s to reduce the number of federal employees, which in turn allowed President Clinton to declare an end to the era of big government. Because the downsizing was almost entirely random, many federal agencies suffered excessive cuts entirely because they had higher separation rates at the bottom of their hierarchies; in other words, more low-level employees quit. Many of the complaints about understaffing are based on the harsh impacts of a decade of unrelenting downsizing.

Once again, there is good news and bad for Defense employees. On the one hand, Defense employees were more likely in 2002 than in 2001 to see enough employees to do the job. In 2001, 46 percent of Defense employees said their organizations always or often provided enough employees; in 2002 the number was up to 55 percent. What is particularly remarkable about this change is that there was no real increase in the number of Defense Department or contractor employees during the period. Either productivity went up or complaining went down, or both.

On the other hand, in 2002 fewer Defense employees said they had enough access to training. In 2001, 34 percent said their organization always provided enough access; in 2002, the number was down to 26 percent. Much as one might attribute this decline to a new urgency about maintaining the edge, Defense employees were clearly telling their leaders that they want more access to the resources necessary to succeed.

Giving federal employees the tools to succeed involves more than just adequate staffing and training. It also means creating the kinds of organizations in which talented employees can see the impact of their work every day. Note, for example, that federal employees were twice as likely as their private sector peers to say there are too many layers between themselves and the top of their agencies. "I have a first-line supervisor," said one employee. "I have a foreman above him. I have an assistant chief above that one, and a chief of the service above that. So, I've got this four-tier operation, where it's hard to get anything accomplished. They could cut out two of those people and spend the money elsewhere."

The layering continues in spite of a 25 percent reduction in the total number of federal managers and supervisors during Vice President Al Gore's "Reinventing Government" campaign. It turns out that many of the cuts were illusory. "We just made believe on paper that the supervisory responsibility was taken away," one federal employee explains. "So I have people working for me who I call team leaders. They can't sign people's time sheets, and they can't sign their evaluations. But I go to them for their input on evaluations and I treat them just like they are supervisors."

Although federal employees were not asked about having enough dollars to do their jobs, the long interviews revealed considerable disquiet about the budget. One of the most passionate complaints came from a lower-level employee who was willing to give up annual bonuses and awards for the money to fix his organization's equipment.

> I could care less about getting an award or getting a bonus. We're kind of back in the hole anyways, so they don't hardly ever remember us except when something breaks down or doesn't cool down or heat up. What I want is to be able to operate my equipment without it constantly failing. . . . It's hard to deal with that when you go to work. You just kind of throw up your hands. Why try? They're not giving me the stuff. We don't have money for equipment right now; we just have to wait until the next budget comes in. You get tired of hearing that.

Rewards

A healthy public service rewards its employees for a job well done, not another year on the job. It measures performance rigorously, disciplines its poor performers, and rewards its stars. It also monitors the overall performance of its agencies and gives them credit for what they do well and holds them accountable for what they do poorly. It is impossible to reward performance, however, if it cannot be or is not carefully, even courageously, measured.

EVALUATING EMPLOYEES.   Federal employees give themselves mixed grades on performance. On the one hand, the 2001 survey showed that all but a handful of federal employees said they do a "very good" or "above average" job.[25] On the other hand, when asked to make their best guess about what percentage of the people they work with are not performing their jobs well, federal employees put the estimate at 22 percent in both 2001 and 2002.

Something does not add up. Either federal employees are vastly over-rating themselves, or they are vastly underrating their colleagues. The an-swer may be in the federal government's performance appraisal system itself, which simultaneously tells each employee that he or she is well above average, while undermining overall confidence that such hyper-inflated ratings could be true.

Of the roughly 700,000 federal employees who were rated in 2001 using a pass-fail system, 92.92 percent passed and just 0.06 percent failed.[26] The rest were not rated. Of the almost 800,000 federal employees who were rated the same year using a five-point system, 43.12 percent were rated as outstanding, 27.56 percent as "exceeds fully successful," 18.45 percent as "fully successful," and just 0.55 percent as either "minimally successful" or "unacceptable." Under either the pass-fail or five-point sys-tem, the federal government has come to rival Lake Wobegon as a home for all those who are above average.

There are three problems in using any of these estimates to determine how well federal employees are actually performing:

—Current law does not allow federal agencies to use a quota system or grading curve in the annual performance process. Although the law is intended to prevent abuse and discrimination, it also weakens the government's ability to raise the bar on performance. Once employees reach the top of the appraisal system, they have no place to go. Moreover, current law also gives federal individual employees ample incentive to fight anything other than an outstanding rating, which in turn leads man-agers to inflate the ratings lest they waste precious time in what has be-come a long and complicated grievance process. Moreover, at least some of the overgrading appears to reflect an effort by managers to protect their employees and departments from downsizing.

—Private employees estimated that there were almost the same num-ber of poor performers in their midst as in the federal government. In 2001, private employees guessed that 26 percent of their co-workers were not doing their jobs well; in 2002, the number was down slightly, to 23

percent. It may very well be that the question about estimated poor performance provokes the same response among all workers—that is, respondents use a normal bell curve to make the estimate.

—Federal employees are much more likely than private employees to
blame the poor performance they see on their organizations than on the
individual. Asked what might explain the poor performance in 2002, 36
percent of federal employees said that their organizations did not ask
enough of the poor performers, 31 percent said the poor performers were
not qualified for their jobs, and 18 percent said the poor performers did
not have the training they need to do their jobs well. All of these percentages were statistically unchanged from 2001.[27]

The question is not whether there is poor performance in federal organizations—or any organizations, for that matter—but what the federal
government can do about it. Unlike the private sector, where nearly half
of employees report that their organizations do a very good or somewhat
good job of disciplining poor performers, the federal disciplinary system
has earned a well-deserved reputation for being overly litigious, confusing, and slow. Asked to explain the general decline in perceived morale,
one federal employee pointed to poor performers: "I can only go by what
I see in my office. But there are people who are troublemakers, but know
they're safe. They make people's lives miserable. They're everywhere. It's
not just in the federal government. They're simply there to collect their
paychecks. They should be disciplined."

According to the long interviews conducted for this report, the problem
is not just on the lower levels. "I think the federal government has too many
managers," one employee argued. "And the working people do all the work,
with very little recognition, low pay, sometimes weird hours, and the managers don't manage anything. They're just there. And it's because their managers didn't want to fire them. Or they had no place to put them."

EVALUATING ORGANIZATIONS. Whatever the difficulties in evaluating
individual performance, federal employees have clear opinions on how
well their own organizations are performing. Unfortunately, their opinions
are decidedly mixed:

—The number of federal employees who said their organizations were
doing very well at running programs and providing services was down 6
percent from 2001 to 2002.

—The number who said their organizations were very good at helping
people was down 7 percent.

—The number who said their organizations were very good at being fair in decisions remained unchanged, as was the number who said their organizations were very good at spending money wisely.

There is one key difference in the ratings between Defense and non-Defense employees: the number of Defense employees who said their organization was very good at helping people did not change between 2001 and 2002, while the number of non-Defense employees who felt the same fell by 9 percent. Non-Defense employees cannot be buoyed by the mission if they do not know just what their mission is.

Trust

Americans continue to have a love-hate relationship with federal employees and the government. On the one hand, the public feels generally favorable toward federal employees and appears to want more of virtually everything the federal government delivers. On the other hand, Americans think federal employees are motivated more by the security and salary than by the chance to accomplish something worthwhile, and they believe substantial numbers are not performing their jobs well.

CONFIDENCE IN FEDERAL EMPLOYEES.   Americans have a distinctly divided opinion of federal employees. According to a May 2002 survey conducted by Princeton Survey Research Associates on behalf of the Center for Public Service, public approval of federal employees hardly changed after September 11. In July 2001, 67 percent of Americans had a very or somewhat favorable opinion of federal government employees; 76 percent did so in October 2001, and 67 percent in July 2001.[28]

At the same time, public views of what motivates federal employees also changed little. As table 5-5 shows, Americans believed the worst about federal employees in July and October 2001 and in May 2002. Forced to choose between pairs of competing explanations for why federal employees join government, the public always focused on the negative.

As table 5-5 also shows, the public is not far off target about the motivations that brought federal employees into government. Where the public might be quite wrong, of course, is what brings federal employees into work every day. They may have come for the security, the paycheck, and the benefits, but a substantial number of federal employees have stayed for the nature of the work.

Regardless of their views of what brought federal workers into government, the public is disquieted at best about the actual performance of

Table 5-5. *What Motivates Federal Employees to Join Government*
Percent

Motivation	Public perception			Federal employees' self-reports 2001
	July 2001	October 2001	May 2002	
Job security (*not* helping people)	70	68	71	65
Salary and benefits (*not* the chance to make a difference)	68	64	71	69
A secure paycheck (*not* the chance to do something worthwhile)	68	63	69	59

government as a whole today. Asked how good a job the federal government is doing running its programs, only 36 percent of Americans said excellent or good, 48 percent said only fair, and 13 percent said poor. By comparison, 40 percent of federal employees said their organizations were doing a very good job running their programs and services, and just 9 percent said their organizations were doing not too well or not at all well. Although the question categories are not exactly comparable, there is obvious disagreement between the two groups.

And this is not the only disagreement. When asked about federal employee performance in early May 2002, the American public estimated that 42 percent of federal employees were not performing their jobs well, a figure that is 20 percent higher than the estimate provided by federal employees (see table 5-6). A month later, another sample of Americans put the figure at 48 percent, no doubt in part because of the continued disclosures regarding the events preceding September 11.[29]

It is important to note that federal employees are not the only workers that Americans believe are underperforming. According to the June 2002 survey, Americans estimated that 42 percent of people who work for business and 39 percent of people who work for charitable organizations are not performing their jobs well either. Americans obviously believe that a great many of their fellow citizens are not pulling their weight at work.

Nevertheless, Americans still look to the federal government as the least effective sector. Whereas 71 percent of Americans had a favorable opinion of charitable organizations, and 65 percent had a favorable opinion of business, just 54 percent had a favorable opinion of the federal government in Washington.

Table 5-6.   *Employees' Estimates of Poor Performance in their Organizations*
Percent

Percent not performing their jobs well	Private sector employees, May 2002	Federal government employees, 2002		
		Governmentwide	Defense	Non-Defense
0	0	7	11	5
1–10	8	35	34	35
11–50	43	47	45	48
Over 50	40	8	6	9
Don't know/refused	9	3	3	3
Average	42	22	20	23

Note: Numbers may not sum to 100 percent because of rounding.

CONFIDENCE IN GOVERNMENT PROGRAMS.   Despite these doubts about employee motivation, Americans still want more of virtually everything the federal government does:

—Only 9 percent of Americans said that federal programs should be cut back greatly to reduce the power of government.

—Forty-three percent of Americans said that government often does a better job than it is given credit for.

—Fifty-six percent said that the bigger problem in government is not that it has the wrong priorities, but that it has the right priorities and runs its programs inefficiently.

When these latter two questions are combined, there is precious little support for radical changes in what the federal government does (see table 5-7). Indeed, from 1997 to 2002, the number of Americans who said that federal government programs should be cut back greatly and that the federal government has the wrong priorities plunged from 16 percent to just 10 percent. During the same period, however, the number who said that federal programs should be maintained to deal with important problems and that the bigger problem in government is inefficiency also dropped, from 39 percent of all respondents to 35 percent, while the number who said that federal programs should be maintained but that government's greater problem is the wrong priorities grew from 14 percent to 17 percent.

Although there is no public constituency for dismantling government, there is a substantial and continuing constituency for reforming it. There is also a smaller, but slightly growing, constituency for winnowing out the wrong priorities. One can argue that this third group is likely to grow

Table 5-7. *Support for Government Reform, 1997 and 2002*
Percent

| Should federal government programs be cut back or maintained? | What is the bigger problem with government? | | | |
| | Has the wrong priorities | | Has the right priorities but runs inefficiently | |
	1997	*2002*	*1997*	*2002*
Cut back to reduce power (1–3 on a 6-point scale)	16	10	22	19
Maintain to deal with important problems (4–6 on a 6-point scale)	14	17	39	35

Note: Data of 1997 are from Paul C. Light, *The True Size of Government* (Brookings, 1999). Numbers do not sum to 100 percent because respondents who answered "don't know" or refused to answer are not included.

the fastest in coming years as the federal government must make tough choices about how to allocate its scarce resources between guns and butter.

These findings fit with general trust in government, which fell somewhat after September 11, but at this writing remains at post-Watergate highs. The number of Americans who said they trust the government in Washington almost always or most of the time rose from 29 percent in July 2001 to 57 percent by October 2001, then fell back to 40 percent in May 2002. These findings also parallel public confidence in presidential appointees. The number of Americans who said appointees are motivated primarily to serve the country rose from just 35 percent in July to 47 percent in October, then fell back to 32 percent in May.

The question is how to reconcile these desires for more of what government does with the persistent cynicism about what motivates federal employees and their leaders. One answer is to become more serious about implementing the Government Performance and Results Act, but using the act as a basis for both rewarding and disciplining performance. Many federal employees rightly complain that the act has become a paper-heavy exercise that does not affect much that matters, meaning budget and personnel.

As noted earlier, the president's budget office recently took an important step toward linking performance to budget. Under the office's proposed guidelines to its own budget analysts, program performance will have a much greater impact on just how much agencies receive each year. It is an important step in the right direction, and could make a significant difference in performance.

At least in 2002, however, many federal employees rightly complained that their organizations were punished for measuring performance. "It was really discouraging for us to get very high marks for having clearly defined, very specific performance goals," one employee remarked in the long interviews conducted for this project. "Then when the goals were not met, we got beat up for having not met the objectives. The vast majority of agencies never came up with clear objectives in the first place. So the lesson was, don't come up with clear objectives because you'll be crucified for them."

Conclusion

The ultimate measure of the health of the federal civil service is whether its employer cares enough to conduct more than the occasional cursory checkup. By that measure, the federal work force is not healthy at all. Its employer does little to track its condition and is reluctant to declare a problem when one exists.

In theory, the U.S. Office of Personnel Management is the logical home for a continuing rating system. It publishes the annual fact book containing work force statistics, has statutory responsibility for regulating the hiring, promotion, and reward system, and maintains the core data files on every employee hired.

In reality, OPM has not shown much interest in rating the health of the work force. It remains primarily focused on making sure that the departments and agencies of government take advantage of available flexibilities to hire and retain the best work force possible.

The General Accounting Office could also build and maintain a rating system, and has shown considerable gumption in declaring the federal government's human capital a "high-risk" area. But the agency eschews rating systems as a matter of course, preferring agency-by-agency analysis to any kind of grand scorecard.

That leaves the task to interest groups such as federal employee unions, good-government groups such as the Council for Excellence in Government, the National Academy of Public Administration, and the Partnership for Public Service, or press outlets such as *Government Executive*, which evaluates agency human resource management through its Federal Performance Project. The problem is that rating systems are expensive to mount and maintain. Without continuous financial support, rating can only be sporadic.

Notes

1. See Paul C. Light, "The Changing Shape of Government," Reform Watch brief (Brookings, October 2000).

2. See Paul C. Light, *Thickening Government: Federal Hierarchy and the Diffusion of Accountability* (Brookings, 1995).

3. National Commission on the Public Service, *Leadership for America, Final Report of the National Commission on the Public Service* (Washington: National Commission on the Public Service, 1989), pp. 11–12.

4. Ibid., p. 2.

5. Ibid., p. 24.

6. Paul C. Light, *Monitoring Government: Inspectors General and the Search for Accountability* (Brookings, 1993).

7. National Commission, p. 39.

8. Ibid., p. 12.

9. Paul C. Light, "To Restore and Renew," *Government Executive*, November 2001, p. 4.

10. George V. Voinovich, "Crisis in the Federal Workforce: Challenges, Strategies, and Opportunities," *Public Manager*, September 1, 2001, p. 5.

11. Senator George V. Voinovich, "Report to the President: The Crisis in Human Capital," Subcommittee on Oversight of Government Management, Restructuring, and the District of Columbia, December 2000.

12. "The Federal Merit Protection Program: Process v. Outcome," U.S. Merit Systems Protection Board, December 2001, p. x.

13. "Mid-Career Hiring in the Federal Government: A Strategy for Change," Partnership for Public Service, February 22, 2002, p. 3.

14. Ibid.

15. George V. Voinovich, "Crisis in the Federal Workforce: Challenges, Strategies, and Opportunities," *Public Manager*, September 1, 2001, p. 5.

16. Paul C. Light, "The Troubled State of the Federal Public Service," Center for Public Service, June 27, 2002.

17. Stephen G. Breyer, "Statement of Stephen G. Breyer, National Commission on the Public Service," July 15, 2002.

18. All comparisons among federal employees in this report involve answers from the same 673 federal employees who were interviewed at two points in time and asked exactly the same questions. Responses were weighted to match the grade levels within the federal government. Tests of sample bias reveal no gender, educational, income, age, race, ethnicity, or agency bias among the 673. This type of back-to-back survey of the same employees is arguably the most powerful tool for detecting change in a population. This study also involved two separate surveys of private sector employees. The first was in May 2001, and the second in January 2002.

19. Paired samples like the one used here involve different tests of statistical significance from the much more common (and less expensive) cross-sectional samples used in most public opinion research. Even small percentage changes in a paired sample can be statistically significant in surveys if the same respondents change their opinions.

20. Employees at other agencies involved in the war on terrorism and homeland security such as the State Department, the Federal Emergency Management Agency, and the Transportation Security Administration may be more like Defense employees than like non-Defense employees. There were simply too few respondents from those agencies to construct a statistically significant comparison. Because they are included in the non-Defense sample, it is possible to infer that the non-Defense numbers are slightly more positive than they would have been had these employees been excluded.

21. This interview was one of forty in-depth telephone conversations conducted with federal employees who had already been interviewed in 2001 and 2002, to discuss trends discovered in the second survey. The interviews were conducted by the Center for Public Service staff.

22. Surveys conducted by Princeton Survey Research Associates on behalf of the Center for Public Service, May 11–June 10, 2001, and January 4–22, 2002. Sample sizes were 500 and 505 respectively, with a margin of error of plus or minus 4 percent for the full sample.

23. These surveys were conducted on behalf of the Center for Public Service, June 18–July 18, 2001; September 27–October 6, 2001; and May 2–11, 2002. Sample sizes were 1,003, 1,033, and 986 respectively, with a margin of error of plus or minus 3 percentage points for each of three cross-sectional samples.

24. As with all the items in the surveys, answers were weighted to represent the grade distribution within the federal government.

25. There was so little variation in these self-appraisals that the Center for Public Service research team decided not to ask the question again in 2002. In all likelihood, the percentages would have remained unchanged.

26. These data come from an analysis of Central Personnel Data File records compiled by the Office of Personnel Management as of December 2001. Their date suggests that the records cover the 2001 performance appraisal process.

27. Private employees explained the poor performance in 2002 as follows: 31 percent said their organizations did not ask enough of the poor performers, 31 percent said the poor performers were not qualified for their jobs; and 21 percent said the poor performers did not have the training to do their jobs well. The question was only asked of respondents who estimated that at least 1 percent of their co-workers were not doing their jobs well. In the federal government 2002 sample, the sample size was 621; in the private sector 2002 sample, the sample size was 425.

28. The survey was conducted by Princeton Survey Research Associates, May 2–11, 2002. The sample size was 986, with a margin of error of plus or minus 3 percent. Previous public opinion surveys were conducted in July and October 2001, with sample sizes of 1,003 and 1,033, respectively.

29. The June survey was conducted by Princeton Survey Research Associates on behalf of the Center for Public Service, June 15–22, 2002. The sample size was 2,820, with a margin of error of plus or minus 3 percent.

SIX

Toward Optimal
Judicial Workways

FRANK M. COFFIN

ROBERT A. KATZMANN

Nowhere in the Constitution is explicit reference made to judicial workways or the conditions of judging. The architects of the charter of nationhood, concerned with the broad design and purposes of institutions, did recognize that the judiciary could not function properly without independence. Alexander Hamilton, quoting Montesquieu, observed in Federalist 78 that "there is no liberty, if the power of judging be not separated from the legislative and executive powers."[1] John Adams wrote that judges should not "be distracted with jarring interests; they should not be dependent upon any man, or body of men."[2]

Judges, then, in the view of the framers, must have decisional autonomy, perhaps the most critical element of judicial independence. Thus, so that they are insulated from public pressure, the Constitution provides for lifetime tenure and prohibits reductions in compensation.[3] Such measures reflect the sensibility that judicial independence would be a hollow, albeit noble, ideal in the absence of conditions that help make decisional autonomy possible. Indeed, over the course of our nation's history, it has become apparent that institutional autonomy is fundamental to a vital

For his invaluable comments the authors express their appreciation to that esteemed scholar-practitioner of judicial administration, Russell Wheeler, deputy director of the Federal Judicial Center. Dominique Welch, judicial assistant to Judge Katzmann, contributed ably to the work of compiling data from the questionnaire discussed in the ensuing pages. We are also grateful to the Federal Judges Association and to its then president, U.S. Circuit Judge Ann C. Williams, for facilitating dissemination of our survey to every Article III judge.

judiciary. That is, if justice is to be dispensed fairly, efficiently, and wisely, then judges must have the time to devote to their responsibilities, both adjudicative and administrative, as well as the necessary resources; and the judiciary must have the authority, within reasonable limits and with appropriate accountability, to manage its own affairs, free of political retribution.

The first of these requirements, time, is in no small measure a function of the caseload. Time, of course, is finite. As A. Leo Levin, a former director of the Federal Judicial Center, noted: "Judicial dispositions are not widgets, and at some point the optimal number of decisions per judge may be exceeded. Productivity cannot be increased indefinitely without loss in the quality of justice."[4] The second of these conditions, resources, has to do with the institutional care and feeding of the judicial office, such as administrative and technological support and law clerk assistance. Another component relates to adequate compensation and benefits, necessary if the judiciary is to attract and retain able persons from diverse backgrounds. A third condition calls for self-governance; that is, judges should have discretion to determine the style of operations in their chambers, and the judiciary, as Gordon Bermant has put it, must have "branch independence" so that, for example, it submits its own budgetary requests to Congress and crafts its own internal rules and regulations.[5] Self-governance recognizes that the other branches have important responsibilities—constitutionally assigned—in such matters as confirmation, appropriations, compensation, structure, and procedure, but that subject to those constraints the judiciary's role is respected.

Time, resources, and self-governance are critical elements of independent decisionmaking. They are also essential components of the optimal conditions for judging. To these may be added another ingredient: work that is challenging and satisfying. Federal courts are designed to be of limited jurisdiction, as forums for the resolution of cases with direct or indirect national implications. If the nature of that work were to broaden significantly beyond these boundaries, the character of the federal courts would also change, almost certainly adversely affecting the capacity to recruit judicial appointees and to retain the services of those already on the bench.

Any informed opinion concerning the optimal conditions for judging and whether the values of decisional and institutional autonomy are honored will necessarily involve answering such basic questions as: Is there time to perform the judicial tasks? Are there adequate resources? Does the character of the work befit the federal judiciary? Is the judiciary self-governing, with sufficient autonomy to resist political pressure? In thinking about how to address such questions, we start with a review of past and present conditions; examine the uses and limits of a variety of workway indicators such as recruitment, compensation, workload, resources, time, resignations, working relationships, security, external institutional relations, public understanding, and media coverage; report on an experiment and survey of judges that combines quantitative and qualitative analyses; and, drawing upon that survey, call for a system of judicial self-help as one way of furthering the objective of optimal judicial workways.

Today's Context

Recent years have seen expressions of concern from a variety of sources about threats to the continued health of the federal judiciary. Recognizing that it is an institution that over the past century has been increasingly called upon to resolve all manner of disputes in ever increasing volume, Chief Justice William Rehnquist provided this snapshot:

> One hundred years ago, there were 108 authorized federal judgeships in the federal Judiciary, consisting of 71 district judgeships, 28 appellate judgeships, and 9 Supreme Court Justices. Today, there are 852—including 655 district judgeships, 179 appellate judgeships and 9 Supreme Court Justices. This past year [1999], over 320,194 cases were filed in federal district courts, over 54,600 in courts of appeals, and over 1,300,000 filings were made in bankruptcy courts alone.[6]

A highly respected senior United States Circuit judge, the former chief judge of the Second Circuit, Wilfred Feinberg, reflecting upon his own lengthy career, noted that in the statistical year 1966–67, the year he joined the Court of Appeals, 979 appeals were filed; he sat on 136 argued or submitted fully and fully briefed appeals; the court had nine active judges and three senior judges; and each circuit judge usually had two clerks. By contrast, in the statistical year ending September 30, 2000, Judge Feinberg remarked that 4,391 appeals were filed, and each active judge sat in about 260 argued or submitted fully briefed cases; the court had thirteen authorized active judges; eight seniors sat frequently with help from many visiting judges from other circuits and from the district courts; and each active judge could have up to four law clerks.[7]

Not surprisingly, given the increasing burdens, the health of the federal judiciary has long been a concern of the third branch itself. For example, at Congress's direction, "Responding to the mounting public and professional concern with the federal courts' congestion, delay, expense and expansion," the Federal Courts Study Committee undertook a fifteen-month examination. Seeking to prevent "the system from being overwhelmed by a rapidly growing and already enormous caseload," the committee warned in 1990 of the "impending crisis of the federal courts."[8] Five years later, the Judicial Conference of the United States approved a "Long Range Plan for the Federal Courts," which observed:

> Today, a number of the federal court's core values are in jeopardy, largely for reasons beyond the courts' control. The increasing atomization of society, its stubborn litigiousness, the breakdown of other institutions, and paradoxically, the very popularity and success of the federal courts, have combined to strain the courts' ability to perform their mission. Huge burdens are now being placed on the federal courts.[9]

Over the past decade, the Year-End Reports of the Chief Justice have been marked with concerns about the increasing federalization of crimes: "The trend to federalize crimes that traditionally have been handled in state courts not only is taxing the Judiciary's resources and affecting its budget needs, but it also threatens to change entirely the nature of our federal system."[10] Another oft-raised problem in the Year-End Reports is that of the adverse impact on the capacity to attract candidates to the bench and retain those confirmed because of inadequate compensation and the failure of judicial salaries to keep pace with inflation. In the words of the Chief Justice: "I fear that . . . the question will not be who is most fit to be chosen, but who is most willing to serve. We cannot afford a judiciary made up primarily of the wealthy."[11]

Still an additional expressed concern relates to alleged congressional efforts to "micromanage the work of the federal judiciary."[12] At the level of the individual circuit judge, one of us wrote:

> There are the pressures to which he or she seeks to respond: an inexorably rising caseload; the demand for expedition in disposing of appeals; the demand to publish all opinions; . . . the rising involvement in administration and committee work; . . . the proliferation of congressional oversight inquiries and hearings often resulting in new

obligations and reporting requirements; the impact of government-wide ethical restraints, limiting judges' recompense from teaching and barring any compensation for delivering a scholarly address or writing a solidly researched article for a periodical.[13]

An esteemed appellate jurist, James L. Oakes, then chief judge of the U.S. Court of Appeals for the Second Circuit, lamented:

> We are merely coping however, because there is very little travel or intercourse among the judges except for those who have senior status, those who are chief judges, or those who serve on Judicial Conference Committees; there are no sabbaticals, and vacations are limited to two or three weeks a year; and there is too little communication among the judges in an age of communication and too little time for meditation in an age of stress.[14]

All judges, we think, understand that any job, even the most fulfilling, is not without some unavoidable frustrations—and for our part, we cannot imagine a life more challenging, more rewarding, or more satisfying than that of a federal judge. But to equate the awareness of a special calling on the part of most judges with a sign that there is no cause for concern would be imprudent. Judges will judge, no matter what the conditions, frustrations, and harassments. But the quality of that judging will suffer. And to the extent that that happens, the nation suffers also.

A Spectrum of Workway Indicators

Before setting forth the authors' concept of ways and means to deal with the expressed concerns, two underlying assumptions should be clearly stated.

The first is that this discussion does not travel under a banner of "crisis." As the distillation of responses of judges in appendix C indicates, among the plethora of specific critical comments can be detected a deep-seated dedication to their occupation. What this chapter proposes is something rather out of the ordinary: the taking of steps to safeguard the optimal effectiveness of an institution *before* diminishing quality becomes a reality.

The second assumption is that the federal judiciary will be able to devise ways to assess and deal with the conditions that threaten quality, which ways are consistent with judicial independence. Federal judges, appropriately, are always alert to any requirement or other action that might encroach on their decisional or institutional autonomy. It would, however, be a poignant paradox if judges were to resist judge-led efforts to identify and monitor conditions that threatened their continued ability to render top-quality judicial service. This chapter therefore assumes that the federal judiciary will be able, in its own and in the nation's interest, to devise the precise means of accomplishing the tasks herein described.

We believe that a multifaceted inquiry can aid in gauging the health of the federal judiciary, the conditions for effective judging. Among the elements to be considered are: recruitment, compensation, workload volume and character, resources, time, resignations, working relationships, security, external institutional relations (Congress and the executive), public understanding, and media coverage. As is obvious, some of these factors are more open to meaningful attempts to measure than others. Quantitative analysis is of limited value for our purposes, however. Rather, we think that periodic qualitative but carefully crafted inquiries, which make use of quantitative data where appropriate, are more likely to bear fruit. The analogy, as is noted in the other chapters in this volume, is to the periodical physical examination, where tests of various types, together with the physician's observations, are combined to mark the patient's status and prospects.[15] While the ability to develop baseline data for the derivation of norms and deviations is far more pronounced in the field of medicine, the discipline of repeated inquiry following consistent procedures is bound to reveal problem areas.

Recruitment

One measure of the judiciary's perceived health is recruitment: whether the judiciary attracts able candidates. Why potential candidates choose not to apply or be considered is very hard to analyze. Identifying such persons presents considerable methodological challenges. The link between recruitment and the conditions of judging is difficult to gauge. Would-be candidates might be dissuaded from applying for reasons completely apart from the judicial environment because, for example, of the nature of the nomination and confirmation processes (a subject itself worthy of continuing scrutiny).[16]

Anecdotal information has occasionally been sought from officials in various administrations who have been involved in screening judicial candidates. A sustained and systematic "exit interview" of such officials over time would yield useful information. Similarly, members of the American

Bar Association Standing Committee on the Federal Judiciary might also be questioned about their views of the recruitment process. And committees organized by various senators to recommend judicial nominees are still another source of experience about the challenges of recruitment.

Compensation

Salary and benefits are easy to track. When they join the bench, judges accept the reality that compensation levels are not likely to rise significantly; public service, after all, is not about financial wealth. But when salary and benefits do not keep pace with inflation, they can deprive judges of stability, a particular problem for those who have young families and the prospect of children of college age. Since 1969, federal judicial salaries have lost 24 percent of their purchasing power.[17] In fact, because living costs differ widely across the nation and judicial salaries are uniform (unlike those of other federal employees who receive locality-based comparability pay increases in high-cost areas), the erosion of purchasing power is even greater in expensive metropolitan areas. Especially for judges living in such areas, the failure of salaries to keep up with inflation affects not just morale, but also their continuing prospects of remaining on the bench, as well as the willingness of potential candidates to be considered for judgeships.[18] The Volcker Commission has endorsed a fresh approach to determining salary comparability by urging that compensation be on a par with that of leading academic and nonprofit centers.[19]

Creation of a permanent, broad-based, and authoritative commission on compensation for the highest levels of the three branches, as proposed by the Judicial Conference Committee on the Judicial Branch, is a sine qua non of any systematic address of this problem. Understanding the uses and limits of such other devices as the Quadrennial Commission on Executive, Legislative, and Judicial Salaries is helpful in considering new approaches.

Workload Volume and Character

Whether and how the volume of the caseload affects judicial performance is worthy of attention. As noted above, volume has increased substantially over time. For many years, the Federal Judicial Center has conducted case weighting analyses, and the Judicial Statistics Subcommittee of the Judicial Conference, aided by the Administrative Office of the U.S. Courts, offers a sense of the burdens on the courts of appeals and the district courts. Russell Wheeler reports that in a 1989 Federal Courts Study Committee survey 58 percent of the circuit judges responded that the extent to which the workload necessitated that they use law clerks for work they should do themselves was "worse" or "much worse" than when they joined the bench. About half of the district judges said the circumstance was about the same, and 39 percent said it was worse or much worse.[20] A 1992 Federal Judicial Center survey, conducted for the Long Range Planning Committee, indicated that nearly 50 percent of circuit judges, but only about 33 percent of the district judges, viewed the volume of civil cases as a large or grave concern, but 75 percent of the circuit judges and nearly 50 percent of the district judges viewed the volume of criminal cases as such.[21] It would be useful to replicate these surveys of judicial perceptions of caseload volume.

The nature of the caseload has changed too, as has the judicial role, in part because of such factors as federalization and sentencing guidelines.[22] The 1992 Federal Judicial Center survey indicates concern among both district and appellate judges about federalization of crimes and their impact on the docket.[23] A study under the aegis of former chief judge of the Southern District of New York, Thomas Griesa, documents the relative decline in the percentage of that court's cases in the commercial and financial area and the sharp increase in the percentage of civil rights cases.[24] With regard to the judicial role, the Administrative Office of the U.S. Courts reported that federal district courts in 1999 completed the fewest number of trials in thirty years, while filings were three times the number in 1969. The number of civil trials has decreased since 1982, and the number of criminal trials has decreased since 1992. In 1980 the proportion of cases terminated by trial in civil cases was 9 percent, but had declined to about 3 percent by 1999; the proportion of criminal cases terminated by trial was 22 percent in 1992, but had dropped to 11 percent by 1999. Systematic examinations of the reasons for these changes and effects of these changes on the judiciary are in order.[25] Periodic inquiries can also be valuable in providing some indication of how the changing nature of the docket affects judges' perceptions of their work.

Apart from issues associated with adjudicative activities, the nonadjudicative component of the judge's work also merits attention. Increasingly, administrative responsibilities occupy the judge at district and circuit court levels, at the Circuit Council level, and at the level of committees of the Judicial Conference. Inexorably, as the size, components, and activities of the federal judiciary have expanded, judges have been compelled to invest their professional time and judgment in addressing the institutional problems facing the judiciary; court administration and case management, uses of technology, updating rules of practice and procedure, interpreting the code of judicial conduct, monitoring budgetary planning and supervising the administration of bankruptcy and magistrate judges' courts, probation, defender services, court security, and other issues. How those duties affect the workways of the judge deserves some inquiry.

Resources

The judiciary's budget is roughly one-fifth of 1 percent of the total appropriated by Congress. Resources are allocated for both the maintenance of the judicial system (for example, providing funds so that jury trials can be conducted) and for support for the judicial office, such as secretarial, administrative, library, technological, continuing education, and law clerk assistance. We would be surprised if judges were unsatisfied with resources provided for the judicial office, although the Budget Committee of the Judicial Conference and the Administrative Office of the U.S. Courts must devote considerable effort to ensure that Congress appropriates adequate funds for the maintenance of the judicial system itself.[26]

TIME.   How time is spent and whether that time is sufficient to perform the judicial task are vital questions, but ones not easily measured. Determining how time is allocated is a labor-intensive task that requires judges to maintain detailed time budgets each day. Perhaps for that reason, only one such inquiry has been undertaken, the landmark Third Circuit Time Study.[27] For a full year the active Third Circuit judges and their law clerks kept detailed daily time records. The average judge's working year exceeded 2,400 productive hours, certainly comparable to the billing hours of most hard-driving law firms. Sixty percent of judge time was devoted to cases; of that, 32 percent was spent on preparation and 48 percent on opinions. Of the almost 40 percent spent on noncase activities, court administration activity accounted for 17 percent of the total recorded judge time, about 5 percent on national Judicial Conference committee work and continuing education, some 8 percent on pro bono community activities, and less than 4 percent on general preparation (embracing all activities necessary to maintain professional competence).

The fact that the Third Circuit study is the only one of its kind ought to be a wake-up call that contemporary studies in the courts—at all levels—should be conducted. There is no better source of information about how judges spend their time and the implications of such. This is an area where some judges resist any external effort to document and analyze their use of time. Their sensitivity is understandable. They do not wish to be assayed against standards they had no responsibility in developing and that may have little relevance to their work. But wholly voluntary efforts designed and implemented by the courts themselves would seem to be a vital tool for coping successfully with present and impending pressures.

Resignations

By themselves, resignation and turnover figures are not necessarily linked to problems of the judicial office. Judges may be committed to serving, regardless of their frustrations. Indeed, the satisfactions of the work may exceed any such concerns. Reasons of health and age could explain departure.[28] Emily Van Tassel and the Federal Judicial Center documented in 1993 that resignation rates were historically low.[29] But troubling signs are emerging. A recent survey indicates that between 1991 and 2000, 52 Article III judges (judges who have lifetime tenure under Article III of the Constitution) resigned or retired from the federal bench, a number that constituted more than 40 percent of the 126 Article III judges who had stepped down from the bench since 1965: 31 of the 52 judges who resigned or retired between 1991 and 2000 joined law firms, and 8 of the 31 judges left before retirement age.[30] Chief Justice Rehnquist reports that more than 70 Article III judges left the bench between 1990 and May 2002, either under the retirement statute or by simply resigning.

Resignations are easy to monitor, and exit interviews with departing judges could yield useful data about the reasons they leave.

Working Relationships

Especially at the appellate level, where decisions are usually made by three-member courts, collegiality is important. The lack of good working relationships would almost certainly impede the functioning of the court. For each circuit, a subjective inquiry into the state of those relationships merits consideration. This is, however, one area where periodic reports attempting to measure collegiality are inappropriate. This is a factor much better addressed under our suggested judicial self-help scenario.

Security

Even before the events of September 11, 2001, the judiciary had been concerned with security; witness the existence of a Judicial Conference

Committee on Security, Space and Facilities. Three judges since 1979 have been murdered while in office, and some judges, such as those who have presided over high-profile terrorism cases, have received round-the-clock protection. It may very well be that the nature of the security issue varies across the country, depending upon the level and type of the perceived threat. The subject is complex, and in the wake of September 11, 2001, we shy away from instant analysis or even the suggestion of appropriate indicators of security. In so noting, we recognize that within the judiciary security is a matter of increasing attention.

External Institutional Relations: Congress and the Executive

In varying ways, Congress and the executive branch affect the institutional health of the judiciary. The executive is charged with making judicial nominations and plays a role in supporting legislation that affects judicial life, ranging from compensation to housekeeping to the substance and procedure of judicial operations.[31] Congress, too, very much affects the courts. The Senate is involved in providing advice and consent to judicial nominees. Congress appropriates funds for the judiciary; enacts legislation affecting the administration of justice by regulating the structure, function, and well-being of the courts; creates judgeships; determines court jurisdiction; sets judicial compensation; passes criminal and civil laws; provides for attorneys' fees; fashions laws that require judicial interpretation; and monitors judicial performance through hearings and surveys.[32] One component of a judicial checkup would involve evaluation of the state of relations among the branches: for example, resources appropriated, judicial vacancies filled, new responsibilities added, criticisms leveled.

Public Understanding

Of all public servants, judges enjoy lifetime tenure so that they are protected from public pressures. But general public understanding of the judiciary is necessary if judges are to make difficult, even unpopular, decisions and have them obeyed. Moreover, legislative and executive support for the maintenance of a vital court system is no doubt affected by public opinion. Thus, measures of general public support could be useful in evaluating optimal conditions for judging. More specifically, individual public complaints against the judiciary might be examined, although such complaints are not especially meaningful in making assessments about the judiciary as a whole.

Public support, however, is not something the judiciary itself can secure. What it can do is enhance public understanding of the job with which it is entrusted. Talks by judges, workshops at courts, open houses—all are means that can be undertaken. Whether a record of such events could be used as a "measure" of understanding, it at least could be used as a measure of effort.

Media Coverage

The public's assessment of the federal judiciary is filtered through media reporting and editorials. An index of media coverage could provide a sense of the state of understanding of the judiciary and hurdles to be overcome in fostering appreciation of the work of the judiciary. Background stories and articles about judicial process are especially productive of understanding. To the extent they can be identified and quantified, their number may supply some indication of the effort made to educate the public.

Beyond Formal Indicators

Data secured from these categories should begin to provide a picture of the judiciary and the conditions of judging. As discussed, quantifiable measures, although useful, cannot by themselves provide a complete picture; indeed, some measures will perforce be of limited value. Rather, what is needed is the richness that qualitative inquiry can provide. Thus we envision that the periodic checkup would involve several steps.

A Process: Four Steps

Step one would be deliberately unfocused, with judges being queried about such matters as what parts of their work experience they find most rewarding, least satisfying, how they spend their time, and what changes would be desirable to improve the functioning of the judiciary.

Step two would involve sifting these responses and creating a more pointed questionnaire in which, for example, judges might be asked to rate the sources of frustration (very frustrating; frustrating; not frustrating) both outside and within the judiciary; to rank order, beginning with the source of the most frustrating, what could be done to improve effectiveness, both inside and outside the judiciary; and to offer their views about how the compensation issue affects the challenge of attracting able persons to the bench and retaining them in office.

Step three would entail focused discussions, based on the responses to the step two questionnaire, perhaps in the context of individual circuit conferences or workshops, with the objective of exploring what kinds of improvements can or should be made within and without the judiciary.

Step four would be the implementation of these suggested improvements. As we indicate under the heading "The Next Step," district courts, circuit courts, circuit conferences, the Administrative Office of the U.S. Courts, and the Federal Judicial Center should be involved in this process.

An Experiment: Views from the Field

Our recent experience provides an example of how such an inquiry might be undertaken. In November 2000 the district and appellate judges of the Second Circuit, with some participation from the district judges of the D.C. Circuit, held a workshop in Cooperstown, New York, under the auspices of the Federal Judicial Center. One of the sessions, organized by present author Robert A. Katzmann, explored "the life of the judge." Along the lines of Step one, the judges were asked a series of general questions. A seasoned panel, consisting of Senior U.S. Circuit Judge Wilfred Feinberg, Senior U.S. Circuit Judge James L. Oakes, Senior U.S. District Judge Leonard Sand, U.S. District Judge Thomas Hogan, and U.S. District Judge Naomi Buchwald, offered their views and engaged in a discussion with the other judges present. Next, the authors of this chapter proceeded to step two, analyzing the responses and devising a more focused questionnaire. Through the good offices of the Federal Judges Association (FJA) and its then president, U.S. Circuit Judge Anne Williams, we were able to send a questionnaire in the FJA newsletter *In Camera*, with return postage provided, to every federal judge. We received 258 responses, nearly 24 percent of the whole judiciary (both active and senior).[33]

The questionnaire and responses (see appendix C) are suggestive of judicial perceptions of a not inconsiderable number of federal judges, although we make no claims of methodological rigor and completeness.[34] The survey results shown in table 6-1 provide a snapshot of judges' frustrations within and outside the judiciary.

If they knew that they could not expect regular cost-of-living increases over the next ten years or a pay raise, 61 percent of circuit judges and 62 percent of district judges would not have applied or would have been less likely to apply. Of those judges in their forties and fifties, again assuming

Table 6-1. *Summary of Judges' Responses to Questionnaire*
Percent of all reporting

Cause	"Very frustrating" and "frustrating"	
	Circuit judges	*District judges*
Inside the judiciary		
Too much work	61	47
Court administration	29	27
Technology	26	24
Case management	19	26
Deliberation	11	17
Personnel	13	15
Outside the judiciary[a]		
Congress	74	
Pro ses[b]	68	
Lawyers	34	
Media	36	
Executive branch	38	

a. Both circuit and district judges responding.
b. Litigants who represent themselves.

no cost-of-living increase or catch-up pay for the next ten years, 64 percent of district judges indicated that it was at least possible that they would
resign; 36 percent said they would be unlikely to do so.[35] The response
rate of circuit judges to this question was too low to draw any meaningful
conclusion.

Insights Provided by Judges' Comments

The FJA response shows a variety of sources of frustration together with
a general affirmation of, appreciation of, and commitment to the profession of a federal judge. The judges expressed widespread dissatisfaction
about: the workload, the level of compensation and failure to keep pace
with the cost of living, the varied actions of Congress (in legislating and in
oversight, but not so much in funding), and the burdens of bureaucracy
and court administration.

Reading the suggestions volunteered by many of the judges opened our
eyes to what a more appropriate forum for self-examination and dialogue
might accomplish. These were not statistics but germs of thought that
invite further probing. A few of them are:

—On the key issue within our control: Learn to work more efficiently.

—On relations with Congress: (a) We need to find more ways to connect with Congress. (b) Invite members of Congress to spend the day with a judge and have judges spend a day with a member. They need to know what we actually do. (c) Give feedback to Congress about how legislation is working out.

—On relations with the executive: Develop relations with the White House chief of staff and counsel.

—On press relations: (a) Get to know editorial writers. (b) Require a court media expert to have media experience, legal knowledge, and good people skills. (c) Hold Federal Judicial Center seminars.

—On lawyers: Assist in their training.

—On relations between appellate and trial courts: (a) Open a dialogue. (b) Eliminate disparate standards of review. (c) Discuss appellate fact-finding. (d) Increase understanding of district judges' concerns (and vice versa?); for example, sensitize judges to the need to shorten opinions and to avoid pedantic reversals and an insensitive tone.

—On administration: (a) There may be too many committees. They tend to be self-aggrandizing over time. (b) A reality check is necessary. (c) Pro ses: Develop more pro se law clerks and staff attorneys; legal assistance for pro ses; clearer rules and procedures; a separate administrative and judicial structure; and less permissiveness toward appeals.

—On technology: (a) "Concern over use of technology to expand production, not improve quality." (b) "Instant communication suggests instant decision." (c) Concern that "rush to endorse technology will lead to unintended advise consequences." (d) For technical training, we need a one-on-one relationship. (e) "Fewer bells and whistles, and more reliability in simpler tasks."

—On easing the workload: (a) Get low-volume courts to help higher-volume courts. (b) Offer sabbaticals. (c) Provide continuing education in case and time management.

Even this list, except for the last entry, does not touch on what judges themselves can do to make their work better and their life more pleasant. One judge responded to the FJA questionnaire with a cry of despair: "I have not taken a Sunday off in two years. I am exhausted, cranky, and disgusted with the failure to adequately staff this court. My 70-hour work week will prompt my resignation." This judge needs help. Probably he or she needs more than just additional staff. The FJA survey and responses indicate that there is a need for a systematic way of addressing problems that will help judges reach their full potential effectiveness.

The Next Step: A System of Judicial Self-Help

Although the survey provided a useful compendium of concerns and suggestions, it did not offer many concrete suggestions. The remedies offered, for the most part, involve actions that only others can take. Indeed, the judiciary could not implement these suggestions, even if it were inclined to do so, without congressional and executive action: for example, repealing newly federalized crimes, diminishing drug cases, abolishing diversity jurisdiction, modifying or repealing the sentencing guidelines, adding more judges, providing for discretionary appeals.[36] For such measures, the judiciary is dependent upon legislative and executive support; hence strategies for strengthening links among the three branches, especially the first and third, are very much in order. Ideas for such approaches could be channeled through the chief judge of the circuit, who, in his or her capacity as a member of the Judicial Conference, could contact the appropriate conference committees.

As to the principal concern about the task of judging—"too much work, not enough time"—the suggestion that judges "learn to work more efficiently" has the virtue of not requiring any ambitious institutional undertaking. The most promising initial step in ascertaining how to accomplish the work with more modulated investments of time should be to draw on the imponderable reservoir, the judges themselves, and get judges to pass on their wisdom and experience to other judges. What we have in mind is a system of judicial self-help.

Perhaps the process of passing on "useful knowledge," as Benjamin Franklin termed it, could begin when a judge is newly appointed. A sitting schedule that places the freshly minted judge on panels with role models is perhaps the most natural way to stimulate thinking about best practices. For judges generally, there are several levels of opportunity within the existing structure of the federal judiciary for the exchange of ideas. One opportunity is the Circuit Conference. Historically, an objective of each circuit conference is to exchange information designed to advance the administration of justice within the circuit. Traditionally, the data and reports are geared to quantitative issues: caseloads, cases and appeals decided or pending, time elapsed between filing and decision, and the like. What we suggest is that periodically, perhaps once every other year, or every three or four years, the Circuit Conference be devoted primarily to sessions, workshops, seminars, focus groups, and simulations designed to present practical problems confronting district and circuit judges (and their dealings with each other).

Such an event might well involve intracircuit initiatives to stimulate informal discussions among the judges on issues of discovery, control, settlement explorations, limiting trial time, use of law clerks, governing complex litigation, opinion writing, sustaining collegiality, en banc proceedings, even the use of a judge's off-bench time. Small workshops within districts and the circuit, undertaken with the assistance of the Federal Judicial Center and the Administrative Office of the U.S. Courts, would prepare the way and identify the agenda, the format, and participants for the conference presentations.

For such programs to be successful, it is essential that the initiative and the direction stem from judges within the circuit. It is not enough to decide on an agenda item and then call in the Administrative Office of the U.S. Courts, the Federal Judicial Center, or other sources of expertise. Each circuit should have a committee or task force of judges whose job it would be to give all necessary guidance in devising and implementing sessions on the quality of judicial life and work. Once the circuits develop some expertise in mounting judge-to-judge self-help events, the U.S. Judicial Conference might well sponsor a cadre of experienced district and circuit mentor-judges to travel where asked and share their wisdom.

In 1989 author Frank Coffin wrote the introductory essay to the *Ohio State Law Journal* series "Judges on Judging" entitled "Grace under Pressure: A Call for Judicial Self-Help." It said in part:

> A threshold question is whether self-help is possible. Do judges have anything that can be given to others? Are such qualities as initiative, a gift for innovation and ingenious improvisation, flair, and intuition communicable?
>
> I recently spent some time with a widely respected judge who had also taught in law school for more than three decades. He was telling me about his teaching a course in negotiating. I asked, "Can this be taught?" His answer was the question, "Can it be learned? If it can be learned it can be taught." Then he quickly added, "Of course not everything can be taught. The basic skills and attitudes and sensitivities can be passed on. There is always something more to it. But this is better than trying to do all of it on the job. Anything that is learned wholly on the job can be improved."[37]

This is what we judges should be doing: learning from our peers what they do and why they do it when their performance of a judicial function rises to such a level of elegance and excellence that it should be emulated by others.

Implementation

This study has focused on the "what" of ways to improve judicial performance. It has not sought information about the "how" of implementation. We now briefly address that question.

We have outlined several areas where a systematic effort at pulse taking can be expected to yield meaningful indications of progress or difficulty in achieving optimum conditions for judicial performance. We have also sketched the fundamentals of a systematic process of judicial self-help.

What is now needed is further judicial input to assess the feasibility of the suggestions and to determine the proper agency for carrying them out. In our view, the obvious body to undertake such tasks is the Judicial Conference Committee on the Judicial Branch. Long concerned with ways to improve the lot of the federal judiciary in such matters as travel and compensation, it has an equal interest in removing barriers to optimum judicial functioning.[38] Its membership also represents all circuits.

Accordingly, we recommend, first, that the projects identified in the section "A Spectrum of Workway Indicators" be accepted by the Judicial Branch Committee for evaluation of their need and feasibility. They include: exit interviews of officials and committees involved in judicial recruitment; analysis of caseload changes and implications; voluntary time studies in district and circuit courts; exit interviews with judges who have resigned; an evaluation of relations among the branches; maintaining a record of judicial efforts to enhance public understanding; and maintaining an index of media coverage.

The committee should seek the aid of the Federal Judicial Center, the Administrative Office of the U.S. Courts, and other committees of the Judicial Conference and would likely find such organizations as the Federal Judges Association, the American Bar Association, the American Judicature Society, and the Governance Institute ready to assist in such an effort.

We recommend, second, that the Judicial Branch Committee undertake to develop a sustained system of judicial self-help involving courts at all levels and all circuits. The concept of judicial self-help should infuse the project from the start. Courts and circuits should be asked for their input. Creative and diverse pilot projects should be encouraged and monitored.

Finally, we recognize that while our focus is on what judges can do for themselves, the effectiveness of the judiciary depends on the successful operation of the entire governmental system. To that end, we reiterate a proposal made some years ago: that a simple entity be created to bring together people in the three branches of government whose common responsibility is working toward the public good.[39] Such an academy could be funded by private foundations, be quasi-governmental (like, for example, the Woodrow Wilson International Center for Scholars), or wholly governmental (such as the General Accounting Office, which monitors government performance). Membership would consist of retired and current representatives of the three branches, scholars, and senior members of the media. Meetings would be convened to periodically evaluate the current state of governing and to identify ways in which it could be improved. The society would assist in the preparation and updating of objective data and surveys of experiences; hold colloquia on the state of governance; issue reports on the health of our institutions and relations among the branches; bestow awards on outstanding performers; communicate concerns to Congress, the executive branch, the judiciary, and the public; and provide comfortable venues for informal discussions and lectures. Such an entity would be a concrete symbol of the governmentwide objective of excellence in the performance of the functions of the three branches.

The far-seeing CEO of even the most currently successful enterprise is constantly seeking better ways to satisfy the public and maintain internal efficiency and morale. The CEO has a reference library of consultants she can call upon. The federal judiciary can use consultants, but only it if can fully appreciate the unique conditions and aspirations governing it. Such an appreciation would be furthered by recourse to its own valuable reservoir of self-help on a wider, more regular, and more systematic basis. What we have proposed is modest and we think eminently doable. Periodic checkups, self-examination, self-help, and the sharing of experiences would be at once preservative and renewing. They would help ensure the continuing vitality of the judiciary and enable its human component, the individual federal judge, to live up to the challenge of enduring excellence.

Notes

1. Alexander Hamilton, quoting Montesquieu, in "Federalist Number 78," in Alexander Hamilton, James Madison, and John Jay, *The Federalist Papers*, ed. and with introduction by Gary Wills (Toronto: Bantam Books, 1982), p. 394.

2. John Adams, "On Government," in *The Works of John Adams*, ed. Charles F. Adams (Little, Brown, 1851–56), p. 181. Gordon Wood notes a competing strain, in which early state constitutions provided for legislative control of courts and judicial tenure; see Gordon Wood, *The Creation of the American Republic, 1776–1987* (University of North Carolina Press, 1969), p. 161.

3. U.S. Constitution, art. III, sec 1.

4. Quoted in M. Tonry and R. Katzmann, eds., *Managing Appeals in Federal Courts* (Federal Judicial Center, 1988), p. 3.

5. Russell Wheeler, "The Emerging Judicial Branch" (Alfred L. Luongo Lecture to the Historical Society of the Eastern District of Pennsylvania), December 11, 1996; and Gordon Bermant and Russell Wheeler, "Federal Judges and the Judicial Branch: Their Independence and Accountability," 46 *Mercer Law Review* 835 (1995); see also Charles Gardner Geyh, "The Origins and History of Federal Judicial Independence," in American Bar Association, Report of the Commission on Separation of Powers and Judicial Independence, "An Independent Judiciary" (Chicago: American Bar Association, July 4, 1997), pp. 81–82.

6. Chief Justice William Rehnquist, "1999 Year-End Report of the Federal Judiciary," p. 1 (www.supremecourtus.gov/publicinfo/year-end/).

7. Remarks of the Honorable Wilfred Feinberg, U.S. Court of Appeals for the Second Circuit at Federal Judicial Center Workshop for Judges of the Second and D.C. Circuits, Cooperstown, New York, November 9–11, 2000, pp. 1–2.

8. *Report of the Federal Courts Study Committee* (April 2, 1990), p. 4. Fifteen years earlier, the Commission on Revision of the Federal Court Appellate System focused on caseload burdens in the appellate courts. Commission on Revision of the Federal Court Appellate System, *Structure and Internal Procedures: Recommendations for Change* (1975), p. 2.

9. Judicial Conference of the United States, *Long Range Plan for the Federal Courts* (December 1995), p. 9.

10. Chief Justice Rehnquist, "The 1998 Year-End Report of the Federal Judiciary," p. 2 (www.supremecourtus.gov/publicinfo/year-end/). See also William W. Schwarzer and Russell R. Wheeler, "On the Federalization of the Administration of Civil and Criminal Justice," Long-Range Planning Series, no. 2 (Federal Judicial Center, 1994).

11. Chief Justice William Rehnquist, "2000 Year-End Report of the Federal Judiciary," p. 2 (www.supremecourtus.gov/publicinfor/year-end/). See also testimony of Justice Stephen G. Breyer and Chief Judge Deanell R. Tacha, U.S. Court of Appeals for the Tenth Circuit, before the National Commission on the Public Service, Washington, D.C., July 15 and July 17, 2002.

12. Chief Justice Rehnquist, "1995 Year-End Report of the Federal Judiciary," *The Third Branch*, vol. 28, no. 1 (1996), p. 3.

13. Frank M. Coffin, "Research for Efficiency and Quality: Review of *Managing Appeals in Federal Courts*," 138 *University of Pennsylvania Law Review* 1865– 66 (1990).

14. James L. Oakes, "Judges on Judging: Grace Notes on 'Grace Notes under Pressure,'" 50 *Ohio State Law Journal* 701 (1989).

15. Remarks of Judge Frank M. Coffin, "Condition for Effective Governance," Governance Institute Colloquium, Woodrow Wilson International Center for Scholars, October 17, 1997, pp. 1– 2.

16. See, for example, *Improving the Process of Appointing Federal Judges: A Report of the Miller Center Commission on the Selection of Federal Judges* (University of Virginia, Miller Center of Public Affairs, 1996).

17. National Commission on the Public Service, *Urgent Business for America: Revitalizing the Federal Government for the 21st Century*, p. 22 (2003) (hereafter the Volcker Commission), available at www.brookings.edu/gs/cps/volcker/reportfinal.pdf.

18. For a different view, see Richard Posner, *The Federal Courts: Challenges and Reform* (Harvard University Press, 1996), p. 30.

19. The Volcker Commission, p. 23. The commission observed that whereas the average salary of federal district judges is approximately $150,000, a recent survey of the average salary of deans of the twenty-five top law schools (as ranked by *U.S. News and World Report*) was $301,639. See also Justice Stephen Breyer, Statement before the National Commission on the Public Service, July 17, 2002 (www.brookings.edu/GS/CPS/Volcker/Testimony/Breyer.pdf). The commission recommended that as its first priority Congress should grant "an immediate and substantial increase in judicial salaries" (Volcker Commission, p. 32).

20. II Federal Courts Study Committee, "Working Papers and Subcommittee Reports" (Additional Miscellaneous Documents), July 1, 1990, p. 4 of the circuit judge report and p. 2 of the district judge report.

21. Federal Judicial Center, *Planning for the Future: Results of a 1992 Federal Judicial Center Survey of United States Judges* (Washington, D.C.: Federal Judicial Center, 1994), pp. 3, 25.

22. On the sentencing guidelines, see, for example, Kate Stith and José A. Cabranes, *Fear of Judging: Sentencing Guidelines in the Federal Courts* (University of Chicago Press, 1998).

23. Federal Judicial Center, *Planning for the Future*, pp. 7, 29.

24. "Study of Trends in Southern District Civil Caseload," prepared by Dwayne Shivnarain for Judge Thomas Griesa, 2000.

25. As to the decline in civil trials, a variety of factors may have contributed, including: civil rules of practice and procedure; views on settlement as a preferred outcome; judicial education programs; case management practices; alternative dispute resolution (ADR) programs; growing workloads, delays, financial incentives for litigants, financial incentives for attorneys; attitudes toward and misconceptions about juries. Reasons for the decline in criminal trials include: sentencing guidelines, a rise in guilty pleas, growing workloads, and prosecutorial strategies.

26. See, generally, Richard S. Arnold, "Money or the Relations of the Judicial Branch with the Other Two Branches, Legislative and Executive," 40 *St. Louis University Law Journal* 19 (1996).

27. "A Summary of the Third Circuit Time Study," in *Managing Appeals in Federal Courts*, p. 299.

28. Statement of William H. Rehnquist, Chief Justice of the United States, before the National Commission on the Public Service, July 15, 2002 (www.supremecourtus.gov/publicinfo/speeches/sp_07-15-02.htm), p. 2.

29. E. Van Tassel, *Why Judges Resign: Influences on Federal Judicial Service, 1789 to 1992* (Federal Judicial Center, 1993)

30. "Federal Judicial Pay Erosion," p. 15

31. See Robert A. Katzmann, "The President and the Federal Courts," in Barry P. Bosworth and others, *Critical Choices* (Brookings, 1989), pp. 131–33. See also "Commentary on Conditions for Effective Governance," pp. 9–10, remarks of Frank M. Coffin presented at the Woodrow Wilson International Center for Scholars calling for the creation of an Academy of Governance encompassing all three branches.

32. The Governance Institute has for many years undertaken work exploring the full range of relationships between Congress and the federal courts. See, for example, Robert A. Katzmann, ed., *Judges and Legislators: Toward Institutional Comity* (Brookings, 1988); Robert A. Katzmann, *Courts and Congress* (Governance Institute/Brookings, 1997). Perhaps the most prominent report of judicial responses to a legislative questionnaire of the judiciary is to be found in U.S. Senate Judiciary Subcommittee on Administrative Oversight and the Courts, "Report on the January 1996 Judicial Survey (Part I, U.S. Courts of Appeals; Part II, U.S. District Courts), May–July 1996 (Grassley Report).

33. At the time of the survey, there were authorized 179 circuit judgeships, 646 district court judgeships, and some 107 vacancies; in addition, 86 circuit judges and 273 district court judges were on senior status.

34. In all, 258 judges responded: 199 district judges; 39 circuit judges; and 20 judges who did not indicate on which court they sat. Percentages are based on the total number of responses to the survey. We note that because some of questions elicited more responses than others, it is difficult to reach any definitive conclusion with respect to those questions. Moreover, to assuage concerns about anonymity, we did not ask respondents to identify their circuits and districts. Had we done so, we would have been able to make comparisons among circuits, geographically and demographically.

35. Specifically, 37 percent indicated "possible," 20 percent indicated "probable," and 7 percent indicated "certain." As for all other judges—those in their sixties and above—15 percent of district judges responded that it was "possible" they would resign, 10 percent that it was "probable," and 5 percent that it was "certain," while 70 percent were certain that they were unlikely to do so. These data are evidence that the closer a judge is to senior status or retirement age, with the attendant financial benefits to be enjoyed upon achieving such status, the less likely it is that he or she will leave the bench, regardless of compensation.

36. Each of these subjects has already generated considerable discussion. For example, on the subject of the size of the judiciary, see Jon O. Newman, "1,000 Judges—The Limit for an Effective Judiciary," *Judicature*, vol. 76 (December–January 1993), p. 187; Gerald Bard Tjoflat, "Commentary: The Federal Judiciary: A Scarce Resource," 27 *Connecticut Law Review* 871 (1995); and J. Harvie Wilkinson III, "The Drawbacks of Growth in the Federal Judiciary," 43 *Emory Law Journal* 1147 (1994). On diversity jurisdiction, see, for instance, Federal Judicial Center, *Planning for the Future: Results of a 1992 Federal Judicial Center Survey of United States Judges* (Federal Judicial Center, 1994), p. 7; Doris K. Sloviter, "A Federal Judge Views Diversity Jurisdiction through the Lens of Federalism," 78 *Virginia Law Review* 1671 (1992); and Frank M. Coffin, "Judicial Gridlock: The Case for Abolishing Diversity Jurisdiction," *Brookings Review*, vol. 10 (Winter 1992), pp. 34–39.

37. Frank M. Coffin, "Grace under Pressure: A Call for Judicial Self-Help," 50 *Ohio State Law Journal* 399, 400 (1989).

38. Indeed, it was at the committee's behest that the Governance Institute began its work on judicial-congressional relations.

39. Remarks of Frank M. Coffin at the Woodrow Wilson International Center for Scholars), pp. 9–10; Katzmann, *Judges and Legislators*, p. 189 (promoting exchanges between the courts and Congress); and Katzmann, *Courts and Congress*, p. 105 (promoting exchanges between the courts and Congress).

SEVEN   *Conclusion: How Do We*
          Get There from Here?

ROGER H. DAVIDSON

This book's premise is that periodic systematic appraisals of federal agencies would be desirable and feasible. We liken them to the periodic medical checkups that many people routinely undergo every year or so. Of course, such checkups are not guaranteed to identify all potential problems or to ensure against subsequent ailments that may require emergency treatment. They do, however, provide a picture of one's general health, pinpoint problems, and provide benchmarks that will aid in dealing with later developments. We have argued that, in like manner, periodic monitoring will broaden awareness and understanding of government entities, both within those entities themselves and among their relevant publics: other federal decisionmakers, organized groups, journalists and commentators, and specialists of all sorts, and interested others.

Our authors have proposed a wide variety of measures of institutional health, some quantitative and others qualitative. No single measure, or type of data, will do the job. Again, the example of medical checkups is instructive. Much of one's health evaluation rests on chemical tests of, say, blood or urine samples, whose results are reported as numerical indicators that can be compared with statistical norms. But equally important are a physician's direct observations and the insights gained in face-to-face interchange between patient and physician. Finally, the patient's history (and often that of family members) forms an important part of the evaluation. Not only do we eschew single or simplistic indicators; we are skeptical also of shorthand reporting devices, such as grades and ratings.

In the preceding chapters we have tried to demonstrate how the various measures we have identified might be applied to government institutions: the House, the Senate, the presidential advisory system, the civil service, and the judiciary. That is, we have attempted "dry runs" employing the types of data we think most useful in reaching conclusions about institutional well-being. In at least two of those institutions—the House and the Senate—large bodies of data are already collected and reported, though not necessarily with the rigor or continuity we would prefer. For the remaining institutions, certain types of data are available only fragmentarily or anecdotally, or not at all. It is virtually impossible, for example, to evaluate the effectiveness of White House staffing and organization in the absence of basic factual information bearing on those matters. So in some cases we have urged new types of data gathering and have speculated about what those data might reveal.

We have presented the intellectual underpinnings for institutional checkups and demonstrated the utility and feasibility of various measuring devices. What remains is to suggest how such a program of checkups might be instituted. Who would gather such information about the target institutions, and who would evaluate and report it? How could existing organizations be enlisted in this enterprise? How would one go about creating new mechanisms for gathering desired data not presently available? Here we suggest some alternative strategies.

A Pluralism of Existing Organizations

An effective monitoring system should adhere to two conditions, as discussed in chapter 1. First, evaluations should be prepared independently of the institution in question, even though these reports may rely in part upon documents, data, and other information generated by the institution itself. Second, the evaluations—however complex and multifaceted they may be—ought to be translated into a form that can be communicated succinctly and meaningfully to relevant publics: those who work within the institution itself, the institution's clients or "relevant others," specialized and mass media, and ultimately the general public.

As public agencies, the branches of our federal government are already the objects of an impressive array of reportage, study, and analysis by an equally diverse cast of characters: individual scholars and journalists, independent organizations, lobbyists, and all manner of political groups. And the institutions themselves produce valuable data concerning their operations, though the data vary in quantity, utility, scope, and regularity of reporting. Most of these institutions use these data to instruct and guide their decisionmakers and employees, and even to embark upon self-improvements. While self-examination and evaluation are rarely sufficient to resolve workways problems, the personnel of the institutions themselves are their greatest assets: they are often more aware of institutional defects than are outsiders, and in any event their compliance must be gained if a process of institutional change is going to work, even if the impetus for change comes from outside the agency.

Congress

The two chambers of Congress are good examples of institutions with built-in corrective mechanisms that may serve to ameliorate some workways problems. As we have noted, Congress all too seldom bestirs itself to study, evaluate, and adjust its operations in any systematic fashion. For each session, however, Congress generates immense volumes of data about its operations that are essential for understanding legislative effectiveness: statistics on the length of sessions, number of bills introduced and acted upon, number of committee meetings, and so forth. These data are published in the *Congressional Record*, in publications of the House and Senate and their committees, and in reports of such support agencies as the Congressional Budget Office and the Congressional Research Service. Institutional memory is the province of the Senate Historian's Office and its House counterpart. The historians' resources include historical records and unique files of oral history interviews gathered from former members and staff aides.

The two chambers have entities charged with disseminating information to new members and counseling members and staffs concerning rules and procedures, most notably, the offices of the Clerk of the House and the Secretary of the Senate, the House Rules and Senate Rules and Administration committees, and the chambers' ethics committees. Moreover, chamber rules and practices can be changed, something that occurs more frequently than one might suppose. The House adopts its rules with each convening of a new Congress; this action is dominated by the majority party, which may make minor or major adjustments in the rules that are normally adopted by a party-line vote. As a continuing body, the Senate faces greater obstacles in amending its rules (a two-thirds majority is required); but changes are not unheard of. And the four party caucuses of conferences (House and Senate Republicans and Democrats) not infrequently change their procedures in ways that affect how the chamber operates.

Independent organizations outside of Capitol Hill publish invaluable compilations of congressional activities. Especially notable are the publications of Congressional Quarterly (*CQ Weekly, CQ Almanacs*, and specialized publications), and the biennial volumes of *Vital Statistics on Congress* edited by Norman J. Ornstein, Thomas E. Mann, and Michael J. Malbin and currently published by the American Enterprise Institute. Data on congressional voting are compiled by scores of interest groups of all kinds, though these compilations are biased in favor of the issues that concern the respective groups. Extensive data on congressional staffs are published biennially in reports of the Congressional Management Foundation.

Scholarly institutions have also been established to promote congressional study and research. In addition to such Washington think tanks as the Brookings Institution and the American Enterprise Institute (AEI), university-based centers include American University's Center for Congressional and Presidential Studies, the University of Oklahoma's Carl Albert Center, and Indiana University's Center for Congress. Other academic centers often include Congress in their scope of research. (Here as elsewhere, the listing is partial; many other groups also perform valuable reporting and assessment functions.)

As for public opinion data concerning Congress (and other branches of the federal government), a variety of reputable nonpartisan organizations are in play. Some survey organizations are associated with universities, some are consortiums with news organizations, and some are independent operations. The Pew Research Center for the People and the Press is a leading example of an independently funded survey organization.

In compiling data on the two houses of Congress, then, we have a plethora of existing resources. What is needed is some sort of central monitoring agency capable of working with several organizations. A first step would be to convene representatives of these entities in order to enlist their joint cooperation in generating reliable, comparable data over time. Assuming that the central agency was adequately funded, it could work cooperatively to nurture existing data-gathering facilities, promote comparable and successive investigations, underwrite new data-collection programs, and develop standards for analyzing and interpreting the results.

The Presidency

Regarding the presidency, the picture is not so clear. The White House as an institution is far less transparent than Capitol Hill agencies, and even basic information about its operations is often extracted only with great effort. Our investigators have set forth an ambitious list of research priorities, beginning with assembling information on White House appointments, staff attributes and turnover, and key structural developments. Among the recommended research techniques are: staff accounts and interviews, surveys of members of the Washington community, retrospective examination of documents and other information, case studies of policymaking, and surveys of the public and institutional "elites."

No existing organization undertakes even a major portion of these research efforts. Certain independent research agencies (such as Brookings and AEI) study aspects of the subject, such as the problems of presidential transition. University-based centers occasionally address problems of presidential management. The University of Virginia's Miller Center of Public Affairs gives special emphasis to the presidency, conducting historical research, compiling oral histories, and sponsoring commissions on public policy issues. There are other organizations dedicated wholly or tangentially to presidential studies, such as the Center for the Study of the Presidency. The presidential libraries—now eleven in number, from Herbert Hoover through Bill Clinton—are the prime repositories of archived materials concerning the modern presidency. They do not normally conduct original research (although several offer grants to scholars and other investigators for specific projects); but they are the keepers of original presidential papers and daily White House diaries, which are available for data collection and interpretation.

The challenge in evaluating White House effectiveness would therefore seem to lie in establishing a research entity that could gather, or attempt to gather, information that is not presently available. (The precise institutional arrangements are open to debate: the new research functions could be undertaken by the central entity mentioned above, or by an infusion of funds to some existing organization, or by a new research group.) The type of research undertaken by investigators Kathryn Dunn Tenpas and Karen Hult needs to be continued and expanded. The techniques they have employed—data gathering and interviewing, for example—ought to be expanded and regularized, so that long-term data on the institution will be available for analysis and comparison. An aggressive, well-funded new research entity would seem to be a logical development.

One question is the degree of cooperation that would be required from the White House establishment itself. In the case of the other institutions we have discussed, data normally can be extracted from public records or compiled from surveys and interviews of elites and the public. The consent of individual respondents would be essential, but institutional constraints are not normally an inhibiting factor. However, the presidency, while superficially the most visible element of our national government, is in fact heavily veiled from public scrutiny and revealed usually under circumstances largely controlled by the White House itself. Staff arrangements and operations under recent presidents have been exceedingly difficult to grasp and analyze, as our authors have noted. The content of staff communications with the chief executive is traditionally regarded as privileged. However, the structure of White House operations and decisionmaking remains an obscure subject, rife with inside-the-Beltway gossip and, occasionally, investigative journalism (the work of Bob Woodward comes to mind). The Clinton administration, for example, fiercely resisted public scrutiny of the formulation of its 1993 health care initiative; the Bush administration was equally adamant about refusing to release lists of individuals consulted in developing its 2001 energy policy and has extended its concern even to the records of former presidents.

Following the example of our authors and other researchers, the proposed agency would be required to scrutinize the public record to uncover information about the White House advisory system. As for releasing data relating to general office personnel and operations—not extending to the content of advice and nature of controversies within the White House—it is simply to be hoped that the prestige, probity, and nonpartisanship of this monitoring agency would persuade presidents to cooperate. Would fear of adverse publicity provide an additional incentive for cooperation? Perhaps.

The Federal Work Force

Monitoring the health of the federal civilian work force—now nearly 2 million employees, not counting contract workers—is an even more daunting challenge. The dedication, morale, and effectiveness of these workers is critical to the federal government's success, whether the goal is collecting taxes, regulating business and industry, distributing Social Security checks, or hunting down terrorists. Unlike the other federal entities we have discussed, however, the "bureaucracy" (all too often prefaced with the adjective "faceless") lacks conspicuous champions, either in or out of government.

There are, to be sure, entities charged with looking after the welfare of federal employees. The Office of Personnel Management (OPM) is the government's central personnel agency. It sets broad standards, administers compensation and benefit programs, and collects data concerning the federal work force. However, current trends (at least since the Clinton-Gore "Reinventing Government" initiatives of the 1990s) move in the direction of decentralizing personnel programs to departments and agencies, a development that promotes flexibility but complicates the task of gathering and interpreting governmentwide data on the work force. The delegation of government tasks to private contractors is another trend that complicates assessment. Although this strategy reputedly results in little savings, it does aid misleading claims of downsizing by removing workers from the public payrolls. This figured prominently in the "Reinventing Government" program and was touted in an ambitious Bush administration proposal involving hundreds of thousands of workers.

At least one prestigious organization, the National Academy of Public Administration (NAPA), monitors the status of the federal service. NAPA's fellows, many of whom are current or former federal managers, periodically forward recommendations to OPM, other executive agencies, and Capitol Hill committees. The Council for Excellence in Government is another organization concerned with improving government performance. Composed of senior public officials and leaders outside government, the council sponsors programs aimed at attracting and retaining talented people for public service and rewarding excellence and innovation in the public sector.

Two Brookings Institution initiatives have cast new light on federal work force problems. One is the Center for Public Service, established in 1999 to investigate three questions: What is the present state of the public service? How can the public sector attract the talent it needs? And how can the public service nourish and utilize the talent it recruits?[1]

Among other projects, the center has implemented the large-scale surveys of federal workers discussed in chapter 5 of this volume. It has also sponsored the second Volcker Commission, an effort to highlight the continuing "quiet crisis" and develop further recommendations for reform. This attention to the plight of civil servants must be maintained, along with the difficult and costly efforts to survey these workers, their managers, and the general public. Ample funding will be required to continue this work, whether through the Center for Public Service or some other entity. These survey efforts need to be replicated periodically and supplemented with economic analyses, in-depth interviews, and case studies. Despite its lack of public and political urgency, this problem has long since reached crisis dimensions and deserves urgent and broad support.

Another effort, the Presidential Appointee Initiative (PAI)—launched before the 2000 presidential transition but continued thereafter—critically examines the process by which high-level presidential appointees are recruited, screened, confirmed, and cared for during their tenure. The PAI's goals are to offer practical assistance to presidential nominees, to identify practical nonpartisan reforms in the appointment process, and to build appreciation for public service. In pursuing its mission, the initiative publishes books and articles and sponsors surveys of past and potential presidential appointees.

The recruitment process for federal political executives—with its array of White House, FBI, and congressional forms and investigations—is duplicative, demeaning, and time-consuming. Many potential federal managers decline to enter this labyrinth. To be sure, government service demands a higher level of accountability than is customary in many private enterprises or professions. But the hurdles potential public servants are required to jump are counterproductive.[2] Moreover, once these appointees reach the nation's capital and are dispatched to their respective assignments in departments and agencies, they are underpaid and all too often neglected and left to fend for themselves; they still represent what a generation ago Hugh Heclo termed "a government of strangers."[3]

The Federal Judiciary

The federal judiciary presents a unique problem for those who propose periodic monitoring. Because judges work and deliberate largely out of the public eye, it is difficult to comprehend the problems they face in the everyday pursuit of their duties. Our investigators not only have relied on their own insights as insiders, but also have canvassed their colleagues and presented what is undoubtedly the most authoritative survey to date of federal judges' views of the problems they confront.

Resources within the federal judicial community are given priority in the process of improving the workways of judges. The Judicial Conference's Committee on the Judicial Branch is the obvious body to identify problems, collect judges' views, and suggest ameliorative courses of action. Basic data on the courts and their workloads are the province of the Administrative Office of the U.S. Courts in the Federal Judicial Center.

Approaching federal judges about these important issues is proposed by our authors as a four-step strategy, embracing: (1) unfocused interviews to identify problem areas; (2) a more precise questionnaire based on the preliminary explorations; (3) exploration of possible improvements arising from focused discussions—perhaps in individual conferences or workshops—and based on the prior two information-gathering steps; and (4) implementation of specific proposals insofar as is possible and practicable.

These procedures are centered within the judicial community itself, in deference to judges' natural resistance to anything resembling outside attempts at influence or interference. And they are premised on the very legitimate view that these methods of self-examination can lead to practical measures of self-help. However, no institutional evaluation would be complete without gathering information and impressions from close external observers: lawyers who have dealt with the courts, the small number of journalists who observe and report on court matters, and knowledgeable observers on Capitol Hill and among government agencies and private interest groups. An unbiased and nonpartisan entity should be charged with evaluating their input, preparing periodic reports on the state of the federal judiciary, and conveying their findings to policymaking bodies, especially the White House, the Justice Department, and House and Senate committees concerned with the third branch.

Monitoring Differing Institutions, Melding Diverse Players

A very large number of organizations already operate within the orbits of the federal government's various branches, scrutinizing their policies and procedures. Many produce valuable information about the operation of government agencies—inevitably partial or self-interested accounts, but nonetheless valuable fragments for understanding and evaluating the workways of government. The future challenge is for an independent entity—rigorous in its standards, nonpartisan in its commitments—to harness and combine these efforts to produce periodic reports on governmental effectiveness. In some cases it will need to devise and implement new (and often costly) procedures for data gathering.

Such a coordinating agency will need to establish a reputation for fairness, nonpartisanship, and a combination of tough-mindedness and sensitivity to the characteristics and constraints of the institutions it examines. Its board of directors must be a diverse group of distinguished citizens representing the several government branches, the scholarly community, and the communications media. Its senior staff of investigators and analysts must command a wide range of research skills, from statistical analysis to historical and organizational exploration. Rigorous standards of nonpartisanship must be maintained throughout. If the organization is to succeed in gaining elite and public attention for its findings, its staff must develop new and attractive ways of presenting and summarizing complex material, and at the same time maintain a personal "passion for anonymity"—a difficult mix of talents.

Such a monitoring agency, in other words, must combine a capacity for leadership and coordination, a financial base that will underpin its initiatives, and a determination to preserve its political and philosophical independence. Political independence may well prove the most vexing: a monitoring agency must be free to render tough-minded judgments, but it must maintain open lines of communication with the practitioners who in the end must implement changes. And such an effort must strive to mobilize opinion makers and the general public, who are all too often uninformed about or indifferent to the workways of government agencies that spell success or failure for our vital common endeavors as a people.

The potential value of such an entity in furthering the effective functioning of our government nonetheless makes the challenge of creating it well worth undertaking. We have sketched only in broad terms the process for designing and implementing these periodic checkups of government health. For our part, however, we—the authors of this volume and the Governance Institute—stand ready to assist the community of concerned organizations, institutions, and citizens in thinking through how best to proceed.

In a real sense, we have been discussing a cutting edge of democracy. The United States has perhaps the most complex, sophisticated, and technologically supported federal government of any democracy. We are confident of the strength of the basic architecture and construction of our national edifice. What has concerned us in this volume is maintaining it: achieving and sustaining the highest quality of service that can reasonably be expected. Our hope is that pursuit of the goal will not be deterred by the enormity of the challenge.

Notes

1. See, for example, Paul C. Light, *The New Public Service* (Brookings, 1999).

2. PAI publications include: G. Calvin Mackenzie, ed., *Innocent until Nominated: The Breakdown of the Presidential Appointments Process* (Brookings, 2001); and G. Calvin Mackenzie, with Michael Hafken, *Scandal Proof: Do Ethics Laws Make Government Ethical?* (Brookings, 2002).

3. Hugh Heclo, *A Government of Strangers* (Brookings, 1977).

APPENDIX A

An Institutional Checkup for the House of Representatives

Representation

Input variables
Member backgrounds, diversity
Mean turnover rates of membership
Mean seniority of members
Proportion of first-term members
Representativeness of committee memberships

Process variables
Mean number of members' committee, subcommittee assignments
Staffing, facilities for district offices
Scheduling of district work periods

Outcome variables
Subject-matter diversity of bills, enactments
Citizens' attitudes concerning House's fairness, representation

Deliberation

Input variables
Size of committees, subcommittees
Clarity of committee jurisdictions
Predictable scheduling of committee sessions
Predictable scheduling of floor business

Qualifications of committee, chamber, and support agency staffs
Compensation, working conditions of staff members

Process variables
Members' time budgets (sample)
Incidence of multiple referrals
Incidence of legislative and oversight hearings
Member participation in committee deliberations
Member participation in floor deliberations
Incidence and types of "special rules"
Incidence of expedited procedures
Number of floor amendments
Timeliness in resolving House-Senate differences on bills

Outcome variables
Balance between work schedules and family obligations
Levels of interpersonal comity during deliberations
Patterns of floor voting
Percentage of bills reported by committees
Percentage of bills enacted into law
Breadth, thoroughness of committee, floor debate
Handling of important (salient) issues

Public Education

Input variables
Availability of Capitol Hill visitors' facilities
Provisions for individual, committee, and chamber publications
Availability of electronic communications

Process variables
Number of Capitol Hill visitors
Circulation of committee and chamber documents
Use of House electronic sites
Level of media coverage

Outcome variables
Number and salience of passed bills and public laws
Public awareness of House proceedings
Public attitudes about performance of the House and its members

An Institutional Checkup for the Senate

Committee stage
Committee assignments per senator
Subcommittee assignments per senator
Number of waivers granted per year
Percentage of salient issues killed in committee

Agenda-setting stage
Outcome of cloture votes
Partisanship on cloture votes
Margin of victory on cloture votes
Frequency of complex time agreements
Time required to negotiate time agreements
Frequency of holds
Outcome of holds

On the chamber floor
Percentage of salient bills passing the chamber (developed in chapter 3)
Percentage of salient bills enacted into law (developed in chapter 3)
Number of quorum votes
Balance of procedural and policy votes cast
Number of cloture votes per measure
Success rates for cloture votes

Bicameral coordination stage
Frequency of conference-related cloture votes

Success rate of conference-related cloture votes
Time elapsed between House and Senate passage and conference
Percentage of salient issues stalemated

"Member enterprise" stage
Senators' time budgets
Senate staff's time budgets
Number of issues on agenda
Number of constitutional demands (treaties, etc.)
Number of constituency-based demands

APPENDIX C

Perceived Obstacles to Performance: Judges' Questionnaire and Responses

Judges' Questionnaire

This brief series of questions seeks to identify obstacles and frustrations perceived by judges in their work and the most likely opportunities for improving our effectiveness. Kindly mail your responses by May 25, if possible, by folding this page in half and stapling the corners.

1. Total years on bench _____; _____ years on federal circuit court;
    ___ yrs. on federal district ct.; ___ yrs. on magistrate ct.;
    ___ yrs. on bankruptcy ct.

2. Rate the sources of frustration experienced in your work:
    V – very frustrating; *F* – frustrating; *NF* – not frustrating.

Outside the Judiciary	*Inside the Judiciary*
____ Lawyers	___Too much work, not enough time
____ Pro ses	___Case management
____ Congress	___Processes of deliberation and opinion writing
____ Public	___Court administration, committees, etc.
____ Media	___Support/personnel
____ Executive branch	___Technology
____ Other (specify)	___Other (specify)

3. Concerning sources *outside* the judiciary:
(a) in rank order, beginning with your *most frustrating*, what can be done to improve our effectiveness?

1._____

2._____

3._____

4._____

4. Concerning sources *inside* the judiciary:
(a) again, beginning with your *most frustrating*, what can be done?

1._____

2._____

3._____

4._____

5. Compensation:
(a) Thinking back to your pre-judicial phase, if you were told that you could not expect regular COLAs over the next ten years or a pay raise, what impact would that have had on your decision to seek judicial appointment?
__Would not apply; __Less likely to apply; __No impact on decision.

(b) Assuming a continuation of bypassing COLAs and catch-up pay for next 10 years:
   (i) For judges in your 40's and 50's, what is the likelihood of your resigning?
   ____Unlikely; ___Possible; ____Probable; ____Certain;
   (ii) All others: Likelihood of your resigning?
   ____Unlikely; ___Possible; ____Probable; ____Certain

Survey Results

Table C-1. *Years of Service on the Bench (Question 1)*
Number, except as indicated

Years of service	Circuit judges	District judges	Court unknown	Total	Percent
1–5	3	38	3	44	17
6–10	6	41	5	52	20
11–15	9	41	2	52	20
16–20	6	37	3	46	18
21–25	7	21	3	31	12
26–30	4	13	0	17	7
31+	4	8	2	14	5
Total	39	199	18	256	

Notes: A total of 258 ballots were returned, two of which did not indicate either years of service or the court. For each question, some number of respondents offered no response.

Table C-2. *Sources and Levels of Frustration, All Respondents (Question 2)*
Percent

Outside factor	Very frustrating	Frustrating	Not frustrating
Lawyers	6	28	58
Pro ses[a]	27	41	23
Congress	37	37	19
Public	<1	7	83
Media	8	28	55
Executive	6	32	52
Other[b]	7	1	4

a. Litigants who represent themselves.
b. Other reported sources of frustration: General Services Administration (GSA); pay; Immigration and Naturalization Service (INS); bureaucracy; Sentencing Commission; the appointment of judges lacking judgment.

Table C-3. *Sources and Levels of Frustration, Circuit Judges (Question 2)*
Percent

Inside factor	Very frustrating	Frustrating	Not frustrating
Too much work	37	24	31
Case management	8	11	59
Deliberation	3	8	67
Court administration	5	24	51
Support/personnel	5	8	69
Technology	5	21	59
Other[a]	3	3	5

a. Other reported sources of frustration: low pay; slow responses from colleagues.

Table C-4. *Sources and Levels of Frustration, District Judges (Question 2)*
Percent

Inside factor	Very frustrating	Frustrating	Not frustrating
Too much work	21	26	47
Case management	3	23	66
Deliberation	3	14	75
Court administration	6	21	66
Support/personnel	3	12	77
Technology	4	20	68
Other[a]	10	4	4

a. Other reported sources of frustration: failure of some to plan/prepare for meetings; time off; low pay; appellate courts/Judicial Council; sentencing guidelines; ideologues on the federal courts; forms and reports; bureaucracy; Judicial Conference; GSA; death penalty cases; CJRA reporting; artificial statistics.

Table C-5. *Sources and Levels of Frustration, Court Unknown (Question 2)*[a]
Percent

Inside factor	Very frustrating	Frustrating	Not frustrating
Too much work	33	33	44
Case management	17	11	78
Deliberation	11	11	83
Court administration	6	39	56
Support/personnel	6	11	89
Technology	17	17	72

a. Twenty respondents.

Table C-6.   *Improving Court Effectiveness: Suggestions Concerning Congress (Question 3)*
Number of judges suggesting

Suggestion or comment	Frustration level of issue[a]		
	No. 1	No. 2	No. 3
Communicate more effectively	18	7	2
Fill vacancies	8	3	1
Restrict federal appellate jurisdiction	2		
Eliminate mandatory sentencing	2	2	1
Eliminate sentencing guidelines	4	5	1
Stop federalizing crimes	3	1	1
Streamline reporting forms	2	1	
Reform ethics law	2		
Delink salaries/pay raises	28	21	5
Restrict federal jurisdiction	8	2	
Write more precise statutes		4	1
Nothing can be done	7	4	1
Take politics out of judiciary	2	1	
Stop attempts to regulate judicial travel			1
Need a new Congress	1	1	
Stand up to Congress	1		
Educate Congress about judicial role	3	5	2
Total	91	57	16

a. An empty cell indicates that there were no responses in that category.

Table C-7.   *Improving Court Effectiveness: Suggestions Concerning Attorneys (Question 3)*
Number of judges suggesting

Suggestion or comment	Frustration level of issue[a]		
	No. 1	No. 2	No. 3
Law schools need to offer more practical courses	8	2	3
Need more professionalism among attorneys	3	2	1
Attorneys need to write better briefs	2		
Not much can be done	2		
Hold attorneys to higher standards	5	1	
Reduce emphasis on hourly billing	1		
Judges should have more control over fees	1		
Judges need more interaction with attorneys	1		
Attorneys need to be better prepared	4	2	
Total	27	7	4

a. An empty cell indicates that there were no responses in that category.

Table C-8. *Improving Court Effectiveness: Suggestions Concerning the Public (Question 3)*
Number of judges suggesting

	Frustration level of issue[a]		
Suggestion or comment	No. 1	No. 2	No. 3
Educate public about the courts	4	2	2
Nothing can be done			1
Total	4	2	3

a. An empty cell indicates that there were no responses in that category.

Table C-9. *Improving Court Effectiveness: Suggestions Concerning the Media (Question 3)*
Number of judges suggesting

	Frustration level of issue[a]		
Suggestion or comment	No. 1	No. 2	No. 3
Improve relations with media	2	2	
Have a court media officer	3	3	1
Educate media about what courts do	6	5	
Nothing can be done	2	1	
Media must improve accuracy of reporting		3	3
Don't talk to media		1	
Allow judiciary to respond to misinformation	2		
Total	15	15	4

a. An empty cell indicates that there were no responses in that category.

Table C-10.   *Improving Court Effectiveness: Judges' Suggestions Concerning Pro Ses (Question 3)*[a]

Number of judges suggesting

Suggestion or comment	Frustration level of issue[b]			
	No. 1	No. 2	No. 3	No. 4
Increase use of pro se law clerks	5	2		
Limit appeal "of right" in pro se cases	1	1		
Increase legal assistance for pro se litigants	9	4	2	4
Stop bending over backward for pro ses	1	1		
Nothing can be done	7	6	2	1
Streamline initial processing of pro ses	7	1		
Require attorneys in every case	2			
Provide education programs for pro ses	2	2	1	
Have more enforceable rules		1		
Create a pro se court	1			
Total	35	18	5	5

a. Pro ses are litigants who represent themselves.
b. An empty cell indicates that there were no responses in that category.

Table C-11.   *Improving Court Effectiveness: Suggestions Concerning the Executive (Question 3)*

Number of judges suggesting

Suggestion or comment	Frustration level of issue[a]			
	No. 1	No. 2	No. 3	No. 4
Reduce the GSA role			1	
Get rid of GSA involvement with courts	4	2	1	1
Improve communication			2	
Educate executive about judiciary role	1	1	3	
Need better buildings and equipment	1	3	1	
Total	6	6	8	1

a. An empty cell indicates that there were no responses in that category.

Table C-12.   *Improving Court Effectiveness from the Inside,*
Circuit Judges (Question 4)
Number of judges suggesting

Suggestion or comment	Frustration level of issue[a]			
	No. 1	*No. 2*	*No. 3*	*No. 4*
Case management				
Congress should limit jurisdiction	4			
Fill judicial vacancies	2	2		
Reduce number of cases assigned per judge	2			
Personnel				
Judges need more support staff	1	1		
Court administration				
Panels should be constituted in a more random way		1		
Deliberation and opinion writing				
Need more collegiality among judges	1		1	
Technology				
Judges need better training	2			1

a. An empty cell indicates that there were no responses in that category.

Table C-13.   *Improving Court Effectiveness from the Inside, District Judges (Question 4)*
Number of judges suggesting

Suggestion or comment	Frustration level of issue[a]			
	No. 1	No. 2	No. 3	No. 4
Case management				
Need more judges/lighter caseloads	22	4	2	
Limit jurisdiction	9			
Either change or abolish guidelines	1	2	1	
Stop micromanaging cases	1			
Cut down on needless reporting	2	2	3	
Stop circuit court interference with district courts	1			
More training by FJC	1	1	1	
Statistical measures need to reflect actual caseload			1	
Limit dispositive motion practice	1			
Enhance judiciary commitment to ADR		1		
Total case management	38	10	8	
Personnel				
Need additional law clerk	13	5		
Pay more to support staff to keep good people	2	2	3	
Allow district courts to hire district executives	1			
Increase training for clerks' office staff	2	2		
Fully fund clerks' offices	1	1		
Hire more staff attorneys for pro se cases		2	1	
Judges should spend less time on employment issues	1			
Judges should have more control when hiring personnel		1		
Total personnel	20	13	4	
Court administration				
Chief judges should learn how to run better meetings	1			
Reduce bureaucracy	2		2	
Nothing can be done	1			
Jurisdiction over matters solely affecting district courts should be returned to courts from the Judicial Council		1	1	
Reduce number of judges' functions	2			
Chief judges should have greater control/authority			1	
Reduce length of chief judge's term		1		
Reduce number of committees	2	1		
Improve communications with Judicial Conference	1			

(continues)

Table C-13. *Improving Court Effectiveness from the Inside, District Judges (Question 4) (Continued)*
Number of judges suggesting

Suggestion or comment	Frustration level of issue[a]			
	No. 1	No. 2	No. 3	No. 4
Take control of courthouses away from GSA	2	1		
Diversify committee appointments wherever possible		1		
Total court administration	11	5	4	
Technology				
Need better training	4		1	
Need better computers and software	3	3		
Need to allocate more funds to technology	2			
Need more up-to-date technology	1	2	1	
Technology needs to be more user-friendly	1			
Nothing can be done		1		
Make all courtrooms adequate for higher technology	1			
Total technology	12	6	2	
Work issues				
Judges need paid sabbaticals		2		
Judges are overworked and stressed	5	2		
Need better dialogue between circuit and district judges			1	
Appeals courts need better understanding of cases	1			
Total work issues	6	4	1	
Deliberation and opinion writing				
Appellate courts should write shorter opinions	1			
Eliminate disparate standards of review		1		
Supreme Court should stop appellate fact-finding by circuits	1			
Circuits should be less credulous in dealing with pro ses		1		
Abolish unpublished or uncitable opinions				1
Need open-minded, rational appellate judges				1
Pedantic reversals and remands by circuits should cease	1		1	1
Need updated courses by FJC			1	
Need fewer opinions and more summary decisions	1	1	1	
Need more time to decide issues and formulate opinions			1	
Total deliberation and opinion writing	4	3	4	3

a. An empty cell indicates that there were no responses in that category.

Table C-14.   *Improving Court Effectiveness from the Inside, Court Unknown (Question 4)*
Number of judges suggesting

Suggestion or comment	Frustration level of issue[a]		
	No. 1	No. 2	No. 3
Case management			
Need more judges/lighter caseloads	6		
Limit jurisdiction	1		
Cut down on needless reporting	1		
Bureaucracy			
Too many committees	1		
Judicial Conference is out of touch	1		1
Technology			
Need better computers and hardware		1	
Need more up-to-date technology	1		
Work issues (except compensation)			
Judges need paid sabbaticals			1

a. An empty cell indicates that there were no responses in that category.

Table C-15.   *Probable Effects on Career Decisions of No Pay Increase for Ten Years (Question 5)*
Number (percent)

Effect	Circuit judges	District judges	Court unknown
Seeking appointment			
Would not apply	11 (28)	37 (18.5)	11 (58)
Less likely to apply	13 (33)	87 (43.5)	5 (26)
No effect	15 (38)	76 (38)	3 (16)
Resignation			
Judges in their 40s and 50s			
Unlikely	4 (67)	35 (36)	3 (37.5)
Possible	2 (33)	36 (37)	3 (37.5)
Probable	0	19 (20)	2 (25)
Certain	0	7 (7)	0
All others			
Unlikely	16 (55)	70 (70)	5 (50)
Possible	4 (14)	15 (15)	2 (20)
Probable	8 (28)	10 (10)	1 (10)
Certain	1 (3)	5 (5)	2 (20)

Contributors

Sarah A. Binder
George Washington University and Brookings Institution

Frank M. Coffin
U.S. Court of Appeals for the First Circuit

Roger H. Davidson
University of Maryland

Karen M. Hult
Virginia Polytechnic Institute and State University

Robert A. Katzmann
U.S. Court of Appeals for the Second Circuit

Paul C. Light
Brookings Institution and New York University

Kathryn Dunn Tenpas
University of Pennsylvania and Brookings Institution

Index